"This book inspired me to make significant life changes. Somewhere deep inside, I knew exactly what I wanted to do. Sophia inspired me to bring it to the surface and move through the fear. It is full of practical advice, tools, and information that will open your eyes."

ERICA OGDEN, WORKING MOM OF 3 EXPERIENCING BURN OUT

"It challenges you…I discovered things about myself — and many things I wanted to share with my daughter, friends, and sisters."

AMY METZ, HARD WORKING PROFESSIONAL, SINGLE MOM OF A TEEN

"It's real, relatable to any age group, and eye-opening."

SHERRY BLAKEMORE, REDISCOVERING HERSELF IN RETIREMENT

"People pleasing is sneaky and creeps in in the subtlest of ways. In this book, Sophia really helps us dismantle our people-pleasing tendencies to bring our most authentic selves forth into the world. I definitely recommend this book to anyone who is stuck in the loop of people pleasing."

IMANI NIC, PATTERN DISRUPTER, MOTHER, ENTREPRENEUR

"A must-read if you're looking to release any guilt around creating the life you truly desire. Sophia's message is about coming back to yourself - it inspires us to rediscover ourselves and find our true calling. This book empowers us to define our favorite selves and live in our truth."

RAYLA MAURIN, CAREER COACH, MAVERICK, INSATIABLE LEARNER

"This book will change lives! It will set people free and free people free people. Nothing is more powerful than stories; through her own story, Sophia guides us through the journey of Unleashing our Favorite Selves. She walks alongside the reader as a fellow sojourner, a temporary resident exploring a space. Sophia provides that space and stays with us in these pages for you and me as we navigate hard places and feelings that have kept us caged."

KATIE SHARER BUTSON, LIFE COACH TO YOUNG ADULTS

unleash your *favorite* self

AWAKEN WHO YOU DESIRE TO BE

SOPHIA HYDE

UNLEASH YOUR FAVORITE SELF:

Awaken Who You Desire to be

Copyright © 2023 by Sophia Hyde

All rights reserved, including the right to reproduce this book or portions thereof in any form whatsoever.

Copyright © 2023 by Sophia Hyde. All rights reserved. This book, or any part thereof, may not be reproduced in any form without the prior written permission of the publisher, except for brief quotations in critical reviews and specific noncommercial uses allowed by copyright law.

For permission requests, please contact the publisher at the address below.

Sophia Hyde, www.sophiahyde.com

PROSE Publishing, www.prosepublishing.com

ISBN: 9798871534328

Printed in the United States of America.

DEDICATION

This book is dedicated to every person in my life who helped me discover my favorite self and develop the confidence that I could help others do the same. Many of you found your way into the pages of this book, but many did not. I recognize that I am the sum total of the people who have loved me and invested in me.

Most of all, I want to thank my loving and supportive husband, Brandon. From believing in me more than anyone else, to challenging me when I was playing too small, to carrying the weight of the household when I had to disappear to write this book, you have always been my biggest fan. Your influence in my life is weaved throughout these pages. My life would be a completely different story without you by my side.

To my two precious children, Eleanora and Liam, thank you for making me a better human. Your presence in my life has changed me and catapulted me into growth I would have never known otherwise. I will spend my life helping you in any way that I can to discover your favorite selves and unleash them into this world. I love you.

To Mom and Dad, thank you. Everything I have done in my life has been made possible and made easier because of the strong foundation you provided me.

CONTENTS

The Favorite Self: 1

Define your Favorite Life: 11

Self-Care: 21

Mind: 38

Body: 59

Spiritual: 79

Financial: 107

Career: 122

Family: 139

Friendship: 159

Contribution: 182

The Blank: 201

Unleash your Favorite Self: 216

References 225

About Sophia Hyde 229

Chapter One:
THE FAVORITE SELF

I have had several crashes in my life, many of which find their way into the subsequent chapters of this book.

Each time I hit another bottom, it felt like I was suffocating.

I felt that way when I ran my body into the ground participating in hustle culture, the term used to make workaholism sound cool and trendy.

I felt that way when I was twenty-seven, moving back into my childhood bedroom with my husband. Our first child was on the way, and we couldn't support ourselves.

I felt that way when I swiped a WIC card for groceries. I thought people who graduated high school with a 6.2 GPA and went to college on a full-ride scholarship were exempt from poverty.

I felt that way when I spent fifteen years trying to lose the same thirty pounds.

I felt that way when I was so miserable as a brand-new mother that my body shut down and physically stopped working.

I felt that way when I was four years into building a business, couldn't make enough to support our family, and simultaneously realized I didn't want to own it anymore. What kind of person quits when they are finally on the verge of success?

I felt that way when I lost friendship after friendship. I mean…I didn't really lose any friends. I just realized, time and time again, that what I thought friendship looked like and what I was experiencing weren't the same things.

I felt that way when I could no longer participate in church after a decade of living with its value systems closely tied to my identity.

I felt that way when I didn't know how to "be" in my own family.

I felt that way when I was filled with hopelessness about the world's problems and my inability to do anything about them.

I felt that way when I suffered in silence.

It was during these pains that I realized what I wanted to be when I grew up…a life coach. Cue the laughter from the audience. There was one teeny, tiny, little problem with this epiphany. My life was a hot mess. I knew I had to solve all these challenges before I could teach others with integrity. I'd spent a decade living in the gap between where my life was and where I craved it to be. I knew what I wanted. I just had no idea how to create it.

Over that decade, I found helpful tools. Slowly but surely, I climbed out of my holes. I paved my own path through a relentlessness, slow burn.

I was born stubborn. I used to think it was a flaw, but now I realize "stubborn" is just a synonym for my tenacity, grit, and intensity. I was determined to find a way to bust out of the boxes I felt trapped inside. The very qualities that made me "too much" for some people were the same qualities that empowered me to keep going.

At the heart of each of them were these core feelings:

- Something isn't right.

- Life is not supposed to be like this.

- I must be doing something wrong.

- I thought I was smarter than this.

- Why are these things (which are easy for others) so incredibly challenging for me?

- Why am I staying stuck?

- I just want to bang my head against the wall. None of this makes sense to me.

Eventually, I figured out how to run a business, mother in a sustainable way, pay off $150,000 of unsecured debt, restore my mental health, build healthy family relationships, find deep spiritual peace, connect with and discover a sustainable healthy relationship with my body, build a stronger marriage, create the friendships I had always craved, make a difference in my community, and simply create a life I enjoyed living.

Life is still very, very messy. The difference between then and now is that I have learned how to hold beauty in one hand and pain in the other.

I reached a point where I felt an overwhelming peace in my life. Once I discovered that I had enough to offer value to others, I decided to enroll in coach training.

A couple of years into my coaching practice, I kept running into the same problem in my conversations. The concepts I wanted to bring together were scattered, either in dozens of different places, or nowhere I could find.

Despite being an avid reader, I resisted envisioning myself as an author. That was for the fancy people with PhDs who were smarter than me and more qualified. I was just a student of the world. Why in the world would I author a book when we are all saturated with so many amazing ones already?

As my frustrations with not having the resources I needed for my clients grew, I finally accepted the reality that I would have to create it myself. I decided to write the book that I craved to recommend.

My frustrations came from gaps in the materials I was consuming. For example, how can you write about having a healthier mind but not address the mental load of motherhood? Most of my female clients are drowning in a sea of tasks. They are exhausted trying to carry the needs of everyone around them while striving to be the glue holding together their families.

What about the crisis facing millions of individuals relating to the lack of a religious home? What effect does that have on someone? How do you find spirituality without religion? How does all of this connect to the marketing companies stealing the term "self-care" and turning it into a sales opportunity for pampering products? Both my male and my female clients were regularly giving from a place of exhaustion and needed new tools. I needed a book that could connect all the dots.

Another one of my frustrations was the phrase "limiting beliefs." It's common coaching jargon describing the concept that we all have beliefs which shape our understanding of the world. However, these beliefs are too often untrue. These beliefs, which are rooted in thoughts, are often subconscious. They significantly shape how we move in the world. We place limitations and glass ceilings on ourselves through our thoughts. Early in my growth journey, I figured out that my thoughts were self-sabotaging. But as a coach once told me, "A picture cannot see its own frame."

Coaches often talk about limiting beliefs, usually as something they can help others identify, but how the hell was I supposed to identify them in myself and reframe them? I couldn't find a method that simplified the concept enough to help me identify my own "limiting beliefs" so I could rewrite them. This frustration motivated me to create my own tools, which I will share with you here.

When discussing personal growth and development, it's common to talk about habits, health, and finances, but what about all this other stuff?

I knew I would never create the success I craved in my business, health, or finances until I addressed the whole picture.

And that, my friends, is why this book was born.

In it, I'm going to lead you through the task of tackling the entire picture of your life.

How do I know this will work? Because I experience it every single day on my coaching calls. Not only did I create a life I thoroughly love for myself, but I've watched my clients do the same for themselves.

My clients are diverse. All genders. They range from teenagers to people navigating retirement. Their financial situations range from a millionaire business owner to a bartender scraping together their monthly payment. They are each unique in race, culture, ethnicity, and religion. These same concepts and materials are working for every single one of them. We are all human. These struggles and triumphs are all part of the human experience. I stand firmly in my belief that we all have so much more in common than what separates us.

And do you want to know the craziest part? Their circumstances rarely changed. They didn't need a new house, new job, new relationship, or million-dollar paycheck to have the life they love. When they come to me, I can see it clear as day. Everything they need is already inside of them. They are already worthy, capable, and qualified enough to attain their desires. They just need help to see it. The same applies to you.

You are already worthy.

You are already enough.

You are already capable.

You are already qualified.

You can attain the desires you have for your life. If you feel like you are suffocating in any area of your life, I hope these pages will help you set yourself free.

Let me make one thing crystal clear, however. The process never ends. It's not possible to write a book about life from the perspective of having "arrived." Half of the healing comes by accepting the reality that it's always going to be 50% hard and 50% beautiful. A significant part of the journey is learning that the "slow burn" is the process. I no longer believe I will ever "arrive."

I've often heard it said that there is no such thing as stagnant. You are either growing or you are dying. It's usually been in a business setting where I have heard this analogy. You cannot just coast. If you are not actively growing your business, then your business is actively dying. There is no such thing as stagnation. This perspective comes from nature. Everything is always in motion. Nothing can ever just stay the same.

However, I see it differently.

We are always growing *and* dying.

Part of the growth process is being willing to release what is no longer working for us. The muscle of learning how to let go is a hard one to grow. It's painful but necessary to prune. Our bodies are constantly shedding dead skin cells and creating new ones. Most trees go through a shedding in autumn, look dead in winter, and reveal their beauty in spring. So too should we be shedding the parts of our lives that are no longer healthy for us.

Naming my work "*Unleash Your Favorite Self*" is intentional. The release is always the first step. Shedding the layers of what is no longer serving you is a significant part of the process. Once you do, you will find a version of yourself more powerful, stronger, and better equipped than you ever imagined.

For most of my clients, the first round of purging is letting go of the expectations that don't align with who they desire to become. I witness people defining their own life terms every day. The words "successful" or "best self" don't sit well with me because they are filled with connotations.

When we hear "success," whether we want to or not, most of us automatically think of financial wealth and material possessions. Without even realizing it, we have ingrained belief systems about being our "best self." We often assume our best must include discipline, a body that's a certain shape, crushing it at the top of our careers, and many other illusions.

Would you confidently say your "best self" spent their entire Sunday laid up on the couch with Netflix and pizza? But what if that's what you find to be the most restorative, joyful activity for you? What language says, "I want to create a life where I can enjoy spending my Sundays on the couch guilt-free if I so desire?" But favorite self? No one can define it but you. The only implication of the word favorite is that you fully own it.

What I know as a fact is that deep inside each of us is a favorite self. A life we crave to live, but it may or may not look like what others seem to want. The only way we will find our peace is if we can remove all the burdens, stories, and expectations sitting on top of us to reveal what's underneath.

My goal for the reader is that by the end of this book, you will have clarity over what you truly want, feel confident in who you are, and feel equipped to take the necessary steps to unleash your favorite self.

These concepts are not to be taken as advice from an expert who can spoon-feed you a perfect meal but rather as an invitation to read someone else's cookbook. You may be inspired to sprinkle in new ingredients and techniques you have yet to try. If you don't care for my recipes, try someone else's cookbook.

I've learned that people are magnets. Sometimes we attract one another, and other times, our energy repels and pushes away. Sometimes, the connection is weak and will barely hold together. Other times, the connection is so strong it requires an intense force to separate the bond. I'm not going to be positively magnetic for every person, nor am I trying to be. However, every time I open the door to let others in, people gravitate to my story and experiences. Many thank me for saying what they needed to hear. Though, admittedly, some say it's not for them.

On Instagram, I've had people tell me they've unfollowed my account because I use too many words, and it hurts their heads to read it all. They have also told me that the content I produce is uninteresting, and they give no energy to thinking about these things. Others have enthusiastically shared, "I've added you as a favorite, so I won't ever miss a post or story you publish. I check every single day to see if you wrote anything new!" The positive impact on those individuals is what keeps me going.

This book is for you. You, who are hungry to hear what it means to be fully human, to be empowered, and to write your own stories. If you decide I don't meet the standard of people you allow to speak into your life, then support authors who do.

Did you catch what I just did there? I just dropped a nugget many of you need.

You are a magnet. If you're struggling with the pain of accepting that not everyone likes you, please stop. Immediately. I beg you. I spent years and years suffering as a people-pleaser. I desperately wanted to be liked by everyone, especially if it was someone I admired. When the sentiment wasn't reciprocated, it was devastating.

Despite years of wishing this didn't bother me and trying not to care, it took learning only one concept to flip the switch. In Ichiro Kishimi and Fumitake Koga's book, *Courage to be Disliked*,[1] they wrote,

"In the teachings of Judaism, one finds the following anecdote: "If there are ten people, one will be someone who criticizes you no matter what you do. This person will come to dislike you, and you will learn to not like him either. Then, there will be two others who accept everything about you and whom you accept too, and you will become close friends with them. The remaining seven people will be neither of these types."

The authors go on to challenge the readers to pay attention to where they give their attention. This simple paragraph completely rocked my world.

The numbers remain consistent whether you allow people to see the real you or let them see the you that's desperately trying to fit in. Whichever version of you shows up in a room will end up with one hater, two admirers, and seven people who don't care. You might as well just be who you truly want to be in this world. It's a hell of a lot easier to find your 20%. Understanding this concept served as a permission slip in my mind. I threw myself into finding my 20%. I started repeating this thought,

"Out of every ten people you meet, one will dislike you, two will love you, and the other seven won't even care. Give all your energy to the two who love you."

I started asking different questions:

- Where are these people?
- How do I find more of them?
- How can I weed out the 10% quicker so they don't bring me down?
- Why am I sitting at a table with the 70%? Am I just a warm body to these people?

For the next twelve chapters, I will be inviting you into my world. If you find we are magnetic, I hope you reach out. If you're in the eight out of ten, it's highly likely you didn't even pick up this book. But if you did, I hope you stay a while and can gain some value from the following pages.

My wish for all of us is to be liberated. I crave to live in a world where we all know our favorite selves, unleash them into the world, and find our two in ten.

Chapter Two:
DEFINE YOUR FAVORITE LIFE

When discussing health issues, we often say we don't want to treat the symptoms only, we want to identify and treat the root cause. However, in other aspects of our lives, we run around chasing symptoms all the time.

In every coaching relationship, my first step is to do an assessment to shed light on both the symptoms and the potential root causes a person comes to me with. The assessment I use is called the *Favorite Life Wheel*.

It's inspired by *The Wheel of Life*, a popular coaching tool that has been around since the 1960s. Paul J. Meyer is credited with popularizing the concept. Since its conception, many coaching systems have released their version of the wheel. Think of each life area as the spoke on a bicycle wheel. One spoke being too low creates a flat tire or a broken wheel, preventing the entire wheel from moving forward.

I was twenty-nine the first time I used a version of the Wheel of Life, and it was a fork-in-the-road moment in my growth. For the four years before that moment, I kept setting the same financial, health, and career goals but saw no progress. I was stuck right in the middle of where I had come from and where I wanted to go. I was frustrated. I felt defeated. Then, I went to a workshop where a life coach led us through an exercise using the wheel, and in a single moment, I saw everything differently. I was able to see that my spiritual and health spokes were extremely low. I discovered the reason my health goals had been stuck for years was because of my mental spoke. The thoughts surrounding how I perceived my body held me back, but more on that in Chapter 5. I finally realized that until I addressed my self-worth and spiritual homelessness, I was going to stay stuck.

I was trying to fix interior issues with hustle, diet, and exercise.

As I improved these areas over the following years, the rest of my life started rolling forward. When I was ready to enroll in coach training, I cross-compared several dozen programs. I wanted to invest in a system I believed could teach me how to deliver tangible results to people. I enrolled in the *Ziglar, Inc. Choose to Win* coaching program. Three years later, I became a Ziglar Master Coach because it centered specifically on the Wheel of Life. The Ziglar organization has been around for several decades. After releasing many books, hosting hundreds of workshops, and working with thousands of people, they examined the common dominators between people who changed their lives and people who learned all the same material, lived similar life circumstances, but stayed stagnant.

After being in the personal growth and development industry for over forty years, they found that the people who changed their lives did so by combining the Wheel of Life with daily habit practices. The rest of this book will break down each spoke on the wheel in detail, and the last chapter will tie habits into this conversation.

The Ziglar Wheel of Life focuses on seven spokes (mental, physical, spiritual, health, personal, career, and finances). The more I worked with clients to help them create significant life changes, the more I uncovered important areas going unaddressed. Hence, the *Favorite Life Wheel* was born. It has ten spokes. Together, in this book, we are going to walk through each of these ten areas of life.

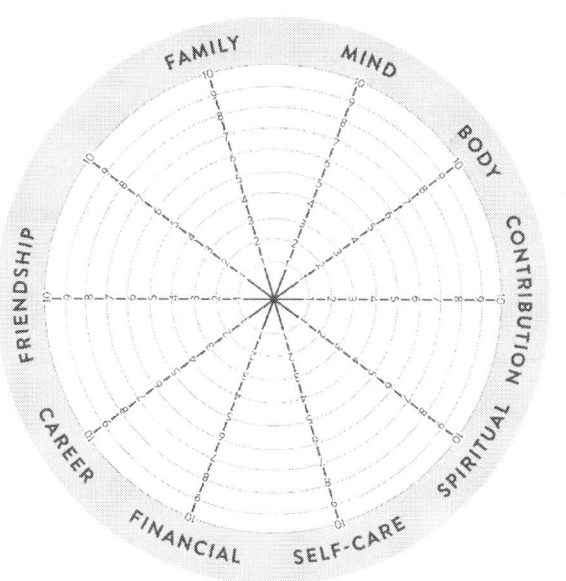

FAVORITE LIFE WHEEL

Spokes: Family, Mind, Body, Contribution, Spiritual, Self-Care, Financial, Career, Friendship

I highly recommend purchasing the companion journal for this book. I will be sharing as many great nuggets with you as I can throughout this book, and it's likely you will walk away with some key takeaways that will inspire you to make positive life changes. However, if you purchased this book because you wanted transformation, you'll also want the journal. When you write, you unlock so much inside of you. Writing not only activates both the left and right sides of the brain and helps you think more clearly, but writing also helps your subconscious come to the conscious level. This book will inspire you, but the journal will open and expand you. I will provide you with journal prompts that will assist you in pulling out the clarity that is inside of you. Most of your birthing process will occur by you answering the questions for yourself.

If you don't have the journal, you can download my app, Favorite Self, and access the assessment there.

I implore you to complete the assessment. I will guide you through it here before moving on to Chapter 3.

Some of you may have done a similar assessment in the past. That's awesome. This exercise is as relevant as a photograph. It shows you exactly where you were at that specific moment in time. But one phone call later in the same day can pull the rug out from underneath you and change everything or deliver you the best news that improves your entire life. I like to run a wheel on myself a few times a year to get a little checkup.

Below, I will walk you through an abbreviated version of the *Favorite Life Wheel* as the rest of the book centers on this foundation. The full version can be found in the journal or on the app.

It is *so important* to go into these steps with no judgment. This exercise may point out some areas of your life that need more work than others. Please note that having a "lack of balance" is the norm. The value of this exercise is not to give you ammunition to criticize yourself, but to help you feel empowered. To improve your quality of life, you must first be aware of what areas need the most attention from you right now.

Step 1: Reflect

Let's begin by getting on the same page. Some of the words on the wheel have different connotations, so I want to make sure we are speaking the same language as we move forward. Take a moment to reflect on these life areas using the provided definitions.

Self-Care- Your ability to manage your energy. Are you giving to others from a place of exhaustion or abundance?

Mind- Includes mental health, thought management, attitude, perspective, knowledge, caring for your brain, and mental rest.

Body- Includes anything to do with your physical health.

Spiritual- Your alignment with your purpose, values, and being connected to something larger than yourself.

Financial- Your money; all the ways you make it, spend it, manage it, protect it, and invest it.

Career- What you're waking up each day to do that creates value in this world.

Family- Some people define the family spoke as immediate family, while others include their extended family members as well. This spoke is not exclusive to blood relatives. Some family is chosen.

Friendship- Your people; however deep, wide, shallow, or narrow you want that list to be.

Contribution- How you are leaving the world a better place.

The Blank Spoke- The last spoke is blank so that you can fill in an area of your life that you want to live with intention but is not currently represented. Some examples could be your partner or romantic life, using this spoke to distinguish between immediate family and extended family, a hobby, your home or environment, your time management, or anything else you want to measure with the intention to empower you to live your favorite life.

Step 2: Define

Using a scale of 1-10, write your definition of a 10 in each of the areas of your life. If you were living your favorite life, what is the most you can dream for yourself in each of the spokes? In the journal and app I share some example definitions of a 1 and a 10 in each area to give you ideas if you need inspiration.

Take time to write out your personal definitions. This is the first step in declaring who your favorite self truly is.

Step 3: Today

Using your definition of a 10, what number on the scale are you at today in each spoke? Write it down next to each definition. Remember, this is as relevant as a photograph. It captures just this moment. It's normal for these numbers to ebb and flow.

Step 4: Connect the Dots

Using the numbers you assigned in Step 3, draw a dot in the proper spot on each spoke. Then, connect the dots together.

Step 5: Learn from Your Shape

If this were a wheel on a bicycle or your car, how well would it roll? Do you have a flat tire? Do you have something that looks more like a star than a wheel? Is your wheel small, with numbers mostly 5 and below? Is your wheel strong, with really high numbers, and just a couple of areas that need a bit of improvement? This visual can offer you powerful insight.

In the next ten chapters, we will dive into each of the spokes, offering different perspectives on how to fill in any gaps you find and get you to where you want to be.

Pictured here is what my life looked like in February 2011, when I hit my first rock bottom and began my growth journey. Also pictured is my life now, in 2022. You can see the difference between the two wheels. The rest of this book will break down the spoke-by-spoke journey of what that expansion over those eleven years looked like.

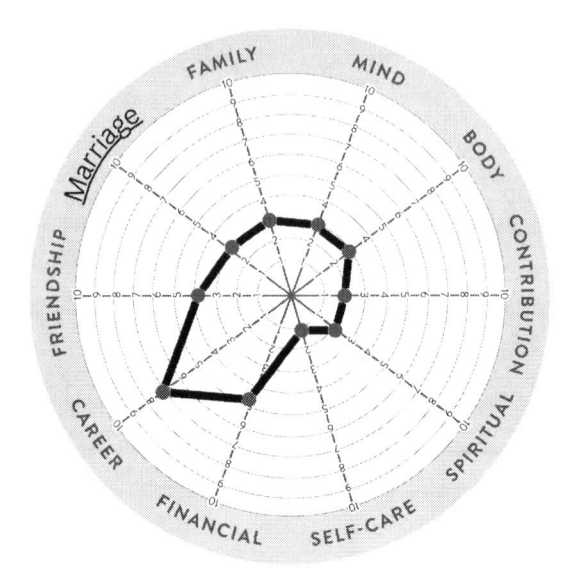

UNLEASH YOUR FAVORITE SELF

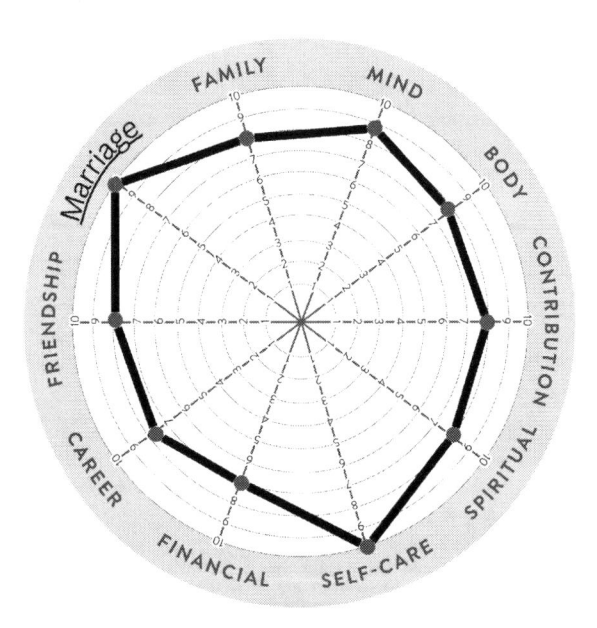

Warning! Don't get caught up in giving too much attention to the wrong gap. Remember to pause and appreciate the gap between where you began and where you are now. For example, if you ranked one of your spokes a 5, this tool shows you two gaps. The gap from 0-5 and the gap from 5-10. The 0-5 gap is worthy of celebrating and acknowledging how much you have done in this area of your life to not be at 0. The gap from 5-10 shows you what work you have left to do. It's important to give yourself a pat on the back for how far you've come instead of only focusing on how far you have left to go.

Habits

After you complete your wheel, the next direction you want to move your attention to is your habits and rituals. Rather than making a task list of what you need to accomplish your goals, a better question would be: What is something small I can do each day to help me improve this spoke?

In chapter thirteen, we will dive into the power of attaching habits to each spoke.

Summary

If you retain nothing else from this chapter about the power of the *Favorite Life Wheel*, soak in this concept: Every spoke is interconnected. That's why they are a circle, not a list. When one area is suffering, other areas will suffer. When one area thrives, other areas will thrive. Before we dive into each of the 10 spokes, make sure you understand the first steps of creating your roadmap.

Clarify Your Destination

The definitions you write for your 10 spokes are yours alone. So often, we get caught up in someone else's definition of what success looks like. When you write out what YOUR favorite life would look like as a 10 in each of these areas, it's like filling in the destination in your map app on your phone. To design a roadmap, you first need to know where you want to go. Your life at all tens becomes your definition of your favorite self.

Define Your Starting Point

Fill out the *Favorite Life Wheel* and get a snapshot of where you are today. Your starting point is your beginning shape.

Decide the First Step of Your Journey

Look at the spoke that was the lowest rated. Reflect on a small habit change you can begin that will create growth in that area. This process is never-ending as our growth never ends. The process is simply to move through each spoke and continue working on new habits that will serve you. Whether by choice or by life circumstances that occur, our wheels are regularly challenged. It's normal to change your definitions and pivot along the way. There is no perfect rhythm of when to redo this exercise. It's a fluid process, so it may change from one week or month to the next. However, the most common recommendation is to review it either quarterly or yearly. Personally, I revisit it anytime I feel off. If I feel like I am lacking clarity or focus, I will pause and check in with myself. I have found the *Favorite Life Wheel* is the best way to look in the mirror and ask myself, "How are you, really?"

Chapter Three:

SELF-CARE

The first of the spokes we're going to dive into is self-care. This is the one I have found to be the most misunderstood. It has incredible power to positively or negatively impact all the other spokes. For most of my clients, we must begin with self-care because the lack of prioritizing their needs is the main cause for the frustrations they are experiencing in their other spokes.

So, what is self-care, exactly?

I define self-care as your ability to manage your energy.

Self-care is not measured by massages, weekend getaways, or the last time you had a pedicure. For some people, these are activities that restore energy. However, for others, these same activities can be exhausting.

Marketing companies realize we're all exhausted, so they advertise products and services to us as "restorative." Yet, most people find they are still burned out shortly after coming home from whatever luxury they've indulged in. Indulgences are a band-aid, not a cure.

The Kitchen Sink

I encourage people to think of self-care as the water flowing from the kitchen sink. The faucet water represents everything you do that fuels you. The water going down the drain represents everything you do for others.

The goal is not to live a life where you aren't giving any of your energy away. That would overflow the sink. Our shared humanity depends on us supporting one another. Life is forever a balance of taking care of yourself and taking care of others. There will always be parts of our lives where we must suck it up and pour out our energy. For me, that's grocery shopping, cooking, dealing with child meltdowns, conflicts with friends or family, and many other parts of my life. Then, there are parts filled with joy that restore me, like meals with my loved ones, cuddling with my kids, making fun memories with my friends and family, going on a walk by myself in nature, reading a book, or listening to a podcast on a long solo drive.

If the water flow represents the giving and receiving of energy, think of yourself as a dish in the sink. Are you a colander? A colander drains the water as soon as it comes in. This would represent someone whose self-care stays empty. They are constantly giving, restoring just enough to keep going.

In my interactions, most people remind me of a measuring cup. It's a constant dance of filling it up and pouring it out. It could look like they go, go, go, Monday through Friday, then crash over the weekend. They recuperate their energy and then pour it all out again.

I encourage people to be an overflowing bowl. Imagine a bowl in the sink where the water pours for so long that it overflows, and the excess water goes down the drain. Technically, they are still giving to others as much as the person who is a colander. However, they aren't empty themselves.

When disaster strikes, who is more equipped to share their energy? The colander has nothing left to give if the water gets cut off. However, the bowl has stored up excess energy. They can keep pouring out to others in time of need because they aren't already empty.

If you focus on taking care of yourself first, then you have more capacity to help others. If you give from a place of emptiness, you will always feel exhausted. You are more likely to grow short with others, become irritated, hit burnout, or implode in frustration if you're at your max.

If you're giving from abundance, you are more equipped to enjoy and sustain that giving. You will have the capacity to stay calm under stress, lead the energy in a room, think clearly, make wise choices, and remain reliable.

Pause and reflect. Ask yourself the following questions. If you had to name your interaction with your self-care practices, are they constant and daily, allowing you to give out of abundance? Are you consistently refueling and emptying yourself? Are you giving out of exhaustion? Which dish analogy represents your life right now?

Hustle Culture

Before I understood self-care, I participated in hustle culture and didn't value rest at all. Hustle culture is prominent in our society, but it's especially common for entrepreneurs who believe that to achieve their dreams, they must work, work, work, and sacrifice whatever it takes to achieve their goals.

I was naturally a workaholic, and then, in my senior year of college, I participated in an intimate interview with an alum from my university who had built a multi-billion-dollar company. He said one of his keys to success was that he works when everyone else sleeps. He said he believes "You can sleep when you're dead." He sleeps four hours a day, never skips a workout, and built his success by working harder than anyone else.

When I decided to admire him and put his advice into action, I forgot to give equal weight to the part where he said he was divorced and his kids didn't like him until they were adults because he was never home and didn't have a relationship with them.

After graduation, my husband and I started a company. I worked a full-time job, and then every evening and weekend, we were building our photography and cinematography enterprise. Our success in the wedding industry took off. I would do bridal consults or edit every evening, and then shoot gigs every weekend. In addition to my hectic work schedule, I was also still involved in community organizations and church.

I remember doing an exercise where I mapped out my calendar for the week. I felt guilty that I couldn't be more productive with the thirty minutes in the morning it took to get ready. My body didn't feel healthy. I once fell asleep in a one-on-one meeting with my boss. I lived in perpetual stress.

The constant dialogue in my mind was that I needed to do more. I should be more productive. I should make more money. I shouldn't rest. It was an insatiable thirst. I created a belief system that nothing I could do would ever be enough to earn rest or pleasure.

Eventually, my body gave out. At a company event, I started crashing. I looked so awful that my boss sent me home. I didn't get out of bed for three days. Sure, you could say I caught a bug, but I know it was my body shutting down from prolonged stress. I was only twenty-four.

Sometimes, this same story plays out much worse. I was lucky I realized at an early age that such a lifestyle was unsustainable. I knew something had to change. I canceled the next week of commitments, stayed home, asked my husband to stay with friends, and deeply reflected on my life. That weeklong sabbatical became a major turning point in my life, which I share in detail in Chapter 6.

Giving Too Much

I know a husband and father who never prioritized himself. He lived for his wife and kids. Everything he did was for them. He made sure they had everything they needed, ran a successful business, took great care of his clients, served his community, and always put himself last. In fact, I'm pretty sure he prided himself on putting himself last. He believed it came from having a servant's heart.

However, that translated to him not taking the time to exercise, eat healthy meals, or develop practices for stress management. Before all his children reached adulthood, he died of a sudden heart attack that was a result of his lifestyle.

If we aren't well, we aren't any good to our friends, families, jobs, or communities.

Glorifying Martyrdom

Our culture worships martyrdom. We glorify the storyline of giving to others at the expense of oneself. In the story about the father, his life fully displayed that he lived for his family and his community, not for himself. But at what expense? Should we really be glorifying self-sacrifice?

Motherhood is synonymous with depleting oneself, being tired all the time, needing a glass of wine at the end of the day to unwind, or not being able to function without all the cups of coffee. This isn't just mothers of little ones, either. Talk to mothers of teens or adults. The conversations around who suffers more will blow your mind. I've had to excuse myself from multiple mom conversations that turn into comparisons of misery.

I don't play that game anymore. Of course, I have hard days, sleepless nights, and mental overload, but operating from a place of exhaustion is not my norm, and I certainly don't brag about it.

So, how do we fix this broken system where self-sacrifice is glorified? The first step is always awareness. We must first take stock of what activities in our lives restore us and which deplete us.

In a moment, I will encourage you to open your journal and write these things down, but first, let's walk through some examples.

Boundaries

When I spend twenty minutes on the phone with a coaching client and they have a breakthrough, I will ride that high for the rest of the day. However, if I take a twenty-minute call from a friend who wants me to listen to them vent, complain, gossip, or criticize, I am spent. If I allow it, those twenty minutes can rob me of my focus and productivity for the rest of the day. Self-care is oftentimes setting boundaries regarding what types of conversations you are willing to participate in and what types you are not.

Boundaries are my favorite form of self-care. How much time can I be around this person before it turns stressful? How late can I stay out before it costs me my energy tomorrow? Who can I be intentional about spending more time around, and who is costing me my peace of mind?

Every time you say yes to one thing, you are saying no to every other priority in your life that could benefit from your attention at that moment. Not standing up for yourself when someone "volunteers" you for something you don't really want to be doing is you telling your family, your self-care practices, or your goals that they aren't as important to you as pleasing that individual.

Understanding our Differences

Let's look at the difference between an introvert and an extrovert. Introverts restore their energy by being alone or with just one or two core people. Extroverts restore their energy by engaging with others. They feed off the energy of other people.

I am an ambivert (both styles) who leans more extroverted. My husband is a solid introvert. One evening, we got home and asked each other how our days had gone. I told him mine was AMAZING. He said it was utterly exhausting, and he would crash early.

It turned out that we both had the same schedule that day, six one-on-one meetings. It took absolutely everything he had to be present with each person and stay "on." By the time he got home, he had nothing left. He was asleep by eight. On the other hand, I was absolutely invigorated by all my conversations. I wanted to tell him all about what I had learned, the new ideas the conversations had inspired, and what I was super excited about. It was a rush of adrenaline for me.

We then applied this knowledge to our lifestyle. I became involved in multiple community groups because that work fueled me. When our daughter was one, I thought it was a good idea to eliminate every commitment in my life except work and family. My husband says it was the hardest year to be married to me. I was not myself at all. We've learned that part of my self-care is community involvement.

He requires lots of time at home, specifically alone, to stay charged. I often go to events by myself. I find friends to be my dates and let him do his thing. At the end of the night, we are both going to bed on a high note. This is part of our self-care practice in meeting each other's needs.

By contrast, ask me to do something that requires detailed focus, which will take every ounce of energy I have. If it involves data entry, chopping vegetables for a meal, or editing on the computer for hours, I'm depleted. I'm capable of managing details, but they exhaust me and take much more time to complete than what most people would need.

Part of our self-care in our marriage is that my husband handles all the grocery shopping and cooking so I can free up that energy. However, I handle all the household management. My phone number goes on every form, and I solve all the conflicts. From calling the doctor's offices to finding someone to repair a broken air conditioner, that's on me. For him, picking up the phone to call a stranger requires massive energy, and for me, it's effortless. For him, grocery shopping and chopping vegetables are just another chore; for me, it's a very stressful experience. As part of my self-care, when he travels for work, the kids and I have charcuterie-like dinners, as in I empty the fridge onto the table and open some rice crackers. My other self-care dinner is to mix oats and protein powder for "chocolate oatmeal."

It will never make sense to me but putting on his headset and playing a video game with his buddies is very restorative for my husband. If he looks particularly drained and exhausted, I'll ask him how long it's been since he's played. Recently, he told me it had been nine days because of work and kid schedules. I could absolutely tell. He was dragging and looked like a shell of himself. I don't understand how gaming is refreshing for him, but he doesn't understand my practices either. I love a ninety-minute massage; he calls that torture. I love to go on a walk or clean the house with a podcast playing in my ears. We both love family movie nights and board games with friends.

Realizing what energizes and depletes us is the first step to getting this spoke back in balance.

Meet Emily

Emily came to me because she was exhausted and drained. She knew the way she was living was unsustainable, but she couldn't bring herself to tell anyone "No." She didn't like the schedule her job required of her. She never had quality time with her boyfriend. She had no time to eat healthily or exercise. She was frustrated and needed a change.

We worked on every spoke in her wheel, but it was the self-care changes she made that set off the domino effect in every other area of her life.

Once she began to understand that taking care of herself was the only way she could sustain helping others, she gained confidence in saying "no." She began to re-evaluate how she spent her time and how much influence others had over her.

Six months later, she had a new role at her company. Her boss started respecting her boundaries and her time. She enjoyed every evening at home with her boyfriend and had time to work out daily. She dedicated Friday nights to planning family get-togethers versus driving around to everyone separately. She didn't feel obligated to run around to meet everyone else's needs anymore. She looked for inventive ways to love everyone in her life and love herself at the same time. I call that a win-win.

Her entire wheel expanded from mostly twos and fours to mostly sevens and nines in six-months.

Surviving

Some of you reading this book may be living in survival mode. You may be thinking there is absolutely no room for you to add time for yourself. But I am here to tell you that you can.

A few scenarios that come to my mind are single parents working as many hours as they can to support their children and trying their best to be present. This could be someone who is caretaking for a family member who is aging or ill, or the mother of a newborn. In situations like these, the idea of having one hour to yourself to do whatever you want feels like an unattainable luxury.

I have clients who are in these seasons, and just getting on a twenty-minute phone call with me requires jumping through fifteen hoops to be alone in their car or closet. Here are a few things they have done to help themselves:

Growing the muscle of asking for help. It feels vulnerable for most of us, but it's necessary. Identify your specific needs so you can communicate them to others.

Find someone in a similar season. One mom started swapping childcare. She takes her friend's kids one night a week, and her friend takes hers. The kids think they're getting a playdate, but it's an opportunity for the moms to have alone time in their homes.

Building pleasure into the day-to-day. Instead of drinking your coffee/tea/water on the go, can you gift yourself five minutes of joy? I recommend that while sipping your drink, pick a thought you can repeat to yourself, such as "I am someone who takes care of myself," "I make pleasure a priority," or "My needs are just as important as theirs." Choose a thought that serves you.

Pausing throughout the day. Sit in the car for five minutes and listen to a favorite song. Slip into the restroom. Just sit there and take a quiet moment for some deep breathing exercises. If you're in there for several minutes, people usually won't ask why.

Set the agenda instead of letting others decide. Rather than asking the family what they want to do, let them know what you are doing because it's what you need. That may be going on a walk/hike because you need to move your body, having a movie marathon because you need to sit on the couch and do nothing for the day, or going on a car ride to nowhere because getting out of the house will help clear your mind. Your needs matter as much as theirs.

Add pleasure into everything you're already doing. Only wear clothes you love. Make your ten-minute showers luxurious with items like a scalp massager or products with your favorite scents. When you buy groceries, buy the ones that give you more energy and feel good in your body. Instead of going on a walk on a treadmill, walk in nature. Rearrange your life to get great sleep. Many of these restorative practices don't require more time but add significant benefits.

Time

One of the most powerful self-care practices you can adopt is to proactively plan your time. The first time I attempted this practice was in 2011 when Michael Hyatt blogged about his *Ideal Week* method. He shared a template of his calendar in an Excel document with the whole week mapped out in thirty-minute increments. He color-coded the blocks based on his priorities. He decided in advance which days and chunks of time are set aside for each area of his life on a weekly basis. He accepts appointments and commitments inside the windows where those priorities belong so that one area of his life doesn't overtake another.

I opened an Excel document and wrote out all the commitments in my life and how much time each week they should be getting to stay healthy. Yeah, that didn't work out too well for me. I was short about 40 hours a week. This eye-opening exercise occurred around the same time I realized my way of life was unsustainable. Priorities like self-care, family, spirituality, and my partner were neglected because my career, hobbies, and friend commitments came first.

How we spend our time reflects what we prioritize.

Fast forward to today, I use my definition of self-care to dictate my calendar. I look at my commitments through a lens of what is required to keep my energy high, and then I plan everything else around that. Yes, it means I decline a lot of opportunities and invitations. I am responsible for taking care of myself and those who are dependent on me. I am not responsible for other people's feelings about my decisions.

My husband and I schedule rest into our lives. We will agree to plans on a Saturday or a Sunday, but not both. One day is always a day at home. We also want to model and teach rest to our children, so we have made some difficult decisions based on the type of lifestyle we want to live.

Since I own my own business, I decided to work about thirty hours a week (except for choosing to write this book, which has been predominantly on evenings and weekends). As I build and grow this business, I want to enjoy my life fully along the way and not live in constant stress. I also have found that when I only have thirty hours, I don't have time for meetings and projects that would be a waste of time or busy work. I choose to think this thought, "I can get more done in thirty focused hours of work because I prioritize what is most effective and efficient. I work smarter, not harder." My husband could have a more predictable income if he went to work for a company full- time, but he chooses to be a freelancer because he can make a livable wage on three to four days of work a week. Last year, our family made more money with both parents working around thirty hours a week than those days before kids when we were both putting in exhausting ten-to-twelve-hour days, six days a week, on a regular basis.

This new way of thinking about time also affects how we parent. For example, when my daughter was two, we enrolled her in dance. She has been bouncing around with a busy schedule ever since. By second grade, our schedules were chaotic, trying to keep up with the competition dance team, Girl Scouts, theater, school events, and more. We said no more. We did not want to normalize at this young age a lifestyle of constant busyness and no rest. Before third grade, we sat down with her, looked at all her interests, and helped her pick her top priorities. We made her release some to provide more rest. In other cases, we were able to pivot to different organizations, providing an outlet for her interests but fewer hours per week. For my son, we've delayed getting him involved in extracurriculars because he's four, in daycare all day, and all he ever asks for is more time at home to play with his toys.

As a society, we have normalized, being busy. "Stayin' busy" has become a common response to the question, "how are you?" Often, when I bump into someone I haven't seen in a while, the conversation will go like this:

Person: "It's great to see you! How have you been?"

Me: "I'm great! So much to be grateful for! How are you?"

Person: "Oh, you know, staying busy. Aren't we all?"

Me: "No. I didn't enjoy living that way, so I am not busy. My life is full of exactly what I want to prioritize, including rest."

I'm about two years into flipping this script, and without fail, it's been jarring to the other person. They have yet to know what to say to me in response. That is how much we have normalized busyness. We run the hamster wheel, believing this must be the only way to exist. I have found that it's a choice. Sometimes, it may be required for a season, but we could set goals that lead us toward a way out.

Does your calendar match your priorities? If not, what changes can you make?

Before I close this train of thought, I want to remind you that comparison is the thief of joy. If you don't see a way around working 60-70 hours a week to provide for your family right now, or something else about your calendar is not in alignment with your favorite life, don't use the story of my family to judge yourself. There's nothing helpful there. If this way of life is something you desire for yourself, then start asking how you can get there one day. What is one step you can take in the right direction? Brandon and I wanted this for ourselves many years ago, created a plan and strategy to make it happen, and then kept charging ahead until we pulled it off. It was not a light switch that we turned on one day.

Escaping

When you reflect on certain ways you may manage your stress, ask yourself whether you are numbing and distracting yourself or doing what is truly restorative.

On my hard days, I may get to the end of the day and begin the mindless scroll on my phone. I may have had intentions for that time, but now I am exhausted. I will find myself sitting on the couch lost in the social media swiping. When I'm done, my energy has not increased. I'm not refueled. I used the phone as a distraction and escape. Social media can add value to my life, but it can also be how I distract from my stress when I could be caring for myself by going to sleep earlier.

This is not self-care. This is escaping.

Watching a show can be pleasurable and restorative for me. Sitting down to watch "*Queer Eye*" or "*Ted Lasso*" is pure joy. I feel refreshed after. Other times, I'm binging some show or rewatching a series from the past to avoid having to think about whatever it is I don't want to deal with that day.

We will be talking about numbing more in-depth in the next chapter, but for now, take note of whether the self-care you're practicing is leaving you feeling restored.

Next Step

Now it's time to go and grab your *Unleash Your Favorite Self Journal* and reflect on this idea for yourself. Turn to the corresponding "Self-Care" section. If you do not have the journal, grab a sheet of paper and make two columns. What leaves you feeling restored? What requires your energy?

Once you have your lists, start with one small baby step. Can you add one habit to restore your energy? Can you cut one thing out of your life that is draining you? Better yet, can you make a swap? Exchange one of those draining habits with a restorative one.

Chapter Four:

MIND

Learning how to manage your mind is the greatest skill you can gain to change your life.

Of all ten spokes, the mind has the most power to pull everything else up with it or drag everything else down as it falls. Understanding how to manage our thoughts and care for our brains is the most significant investment we can make in ourselves.

The mind spoke includes the ability to:

- Manage Your Thoughts
- Choose Your Attitude
- See Different Perspectives
- Accumulate Knowledge
- Care for Your Brain
- Your Mental Health
- Rest Your Mind

Own Your Power

Many of you have heard of victim mentality - when an individual blames other people for their problems. It's widely taught that the key to combating victim mentality is taking personal responsibility. Grasping this concept and deciding to fully own every interaction, conversation, situation, and event in my life was one of the most empowering tools I have ever learned.

However, I don't teach victim mentality versus personal responsibility. It's not a healthy perspective in every situation.

Recently, I was at an event and this businessman went off on a riff about how the biggest problem with our world is that everyone has a victim mentality, and they feel entitled to have other people fix their problems. Is there an abundance of people blaming others for their problems? Sure, but also, isn't there an abundance of people with power making crappy decisions that affect millions of people's lives? Also, yes.

Unfortunately, taken to an extreme, victim mentality can be used to make actual victims of other people's mistakes believe something is their fault when it is not. They're just left cleaning up the mess.

The alternative language I use is to encourage others to "take your power back." Focus on what you can control and release the rest. This allows us to name an injustice without letting it consume us.

I have a client who inspires me every single time we connect. She is the mother of four young children going through a divorce whose ex-husband is constantly sabotaging her efforts to stand on her own two feet. She had to leave the marriage because of his manipulative, abusive behaviors. After he cut off her financial access to the business they built together, she started a new one from the ground up to generate income. Of course, it's hard. Of course, she's tired. However, she is always taking control of the actions within her power and moving to the next thing that will push her forward to her goals.

On the hard days, when his actions feel like he's cutting her off at the knees once again, our conversations always center around separating what is not her fault from what is in her control.

When we can name the event, circumstance, or problem as an injustice, that is not claiming victimhood. It's asserting that a wrong has occurred. STAYING there is the problem. I always encourage my clients to go back to what is always in our control:

- Our thoughts
- Our feelings
- Our words
- Our actions

We cannot control others' thoughts, words, actions, or feelings, but we can control ours. When we fully grasp that concept, we can take our power back.

Limiting Beliefs

When I first started diving into the personal growth and development world, I found the phrase "limiting beliefs" all over the place.

The concept of a limiting belief is that we hold ourselves back. We have thoughts in our minds that our brains perceive as facts. However, they are not facts. They are opinions, thoughts, stories, or malleable ideas.

I'll give you an example of a limiting belief using my inspirational friend, Angelica. Angelica was the daughter of migrant workers and quit school at twelve years old to help pick strawberries and support the family. She didn't believe she was worthy of a high school diploma because no one around her had one. Therefore, she believed this was how "people like her" lived.

By her mid-twenties, she had two children and was still in the fields. She enrolled in a literacy program, and the teacher told her, "I think you can get a GED." WHAT? Her limiting belief was that she could not get an education. And then she achieved it. Her mentor then told her, "I think you can get into community college." WHAT? There was another limiting belief, "People like me don't go to college." After her associate degree, her mentor said, "I think you can get a four-year degree." WHAT? Her limiting beliefs never allowed her to dream of having a degree. Sure enough, she got into the local state university and graduated with a bachelor's degree. Angelica got a new career, met her husband, and built an entire life - one she had once believed was beyond her reach. She now runs a successful literacy non-profit, where she helps others believe in their potential too.

Many of Angelica's limiting beliefs were that people "like her" couldn't have many things in life that many of you reading this book never questioned for yourself. Her story may be different from your story, but every single one of us have thoughts that limit us.

Changing our thoughts is undeniably the most powerful way to change our lives.

The Thought Wheel

As I tried to pursue my growth, get unstuck, and get out of my own way, I kept running into the same major issue. How the hell do I discover what these so-called "limiting beliefs" are? Sure, I could hire a coach, and the ones I have are awesome at naming thoughts I couldn't see. However, I wanted to be able to do this for myself on a random evening in my home when I was feeling a little off.

After studying several tools from different coaching and psychology practices, it still felt complicated for my brain. I finally just sat down and merged several concepts into one document, that allowed me to walk through a process that worked. I needed a simple format that would allow me to look at my own thoughts.

Before diving into the tool and how I apply it, let's look at the basic tenets that inspired me. Cognitive Behavioral Therapy is a well-researched form of therapy, based on the theory that what we think creates how we feel. How we feel influences how we behave. And how we behave reinforces what we think. Put in layman's terms, change your thoughts, change your life. CBT-trained therapists use this technique to treat issues ranging from eating disorders to anxiety and depression and so much more.

There are many systems in the world that help people learn to manage their thoughts, but I couldn't find one that resonated with me personally.

Eventually, I realized I needed journal prompts that would help me take pen to paper to unlock what was sitting underneath the surface. As I mentioned earlier, journaling is immensely powerful, and I wanted a way to tap into my inner world more easily.

So, I designed a simple tool called *The Thought Wheel.*

The Thought Wheel is a series of questions you can ask yourself that allow you to reflect on what you're thinking, get to the bottom of where the thoughts came from, and then consciously choose to rewrite new thoughts and actions that will serve you.

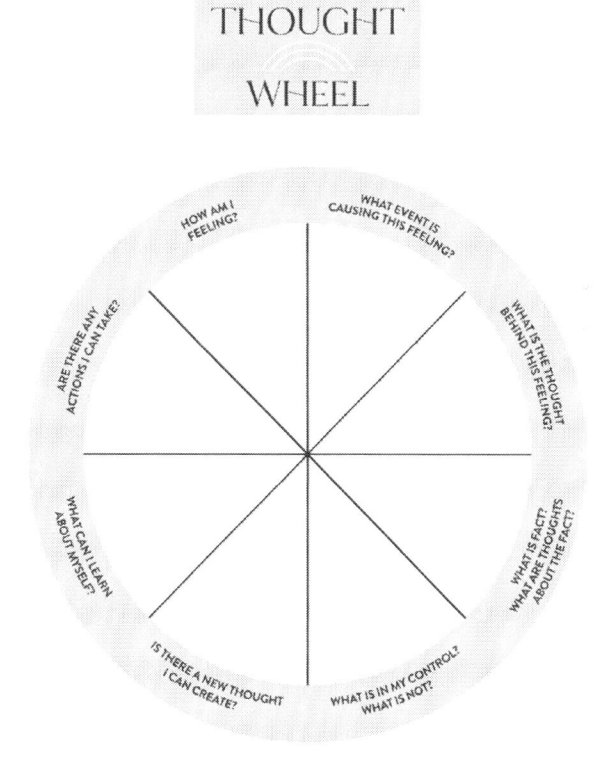

THOUGHT WHEEL

- HOW AM I FEELING?
- WHAT EVENT IS CAUSING THIS FEELING?
- WHAT IS THE THOUGHT BEHIND THIS FEELING?
- WHAT IS FACT? WHAT ARE THOUGHTS ABOUT THE FACT?
- WHAT IS IN MY CONTROL? WHAT IS NOT?
- IS THERE A NEW THOUGHT I CAN CREATE?
- WHAT CAN I LEARN ABOUT MYSELF?
- ARE THERE ANY ACTIONS I CAN TAKE?

When I use this tool, I open a journal and use each of these questions as a prompt. It's amazing what writing can bring out of your body, mind, and soul that you didn't realize you were holding inside.

The reason I designed it as a wheel was to give you the ability to choose any starting point. The easiest and most common entry point is the question, "How am I feeling?" But depending on the situation, you can start anywhere in the process.

In the app, I have recorded a tutorial on how to use this tool.

More than any other tool in any spoke of my coaching system, The Thought Wheel has helped people transform their lives the most. It simultaneously teaches people how to feel their feelings and unlock new ways of thinking that will serve them better.

Escaping

In the self-care chapter, I mentioned that we often escape, distract, or numb when we feel uncomfortable. This can manifest in a plethora of ways.

Personally, this looks like a 10:00 p.m. bowl of ice cream. For others, it's binging TV, scrolling social media, alcohol, drugs, sex, porn, overeating, or even excessive exercise. Ice cream is not bad, especially when consumed for joy and pleasure. However, when this, or any escaping tactic, is used to numb feelings, it may be time to look at what's happening beneath the surface.

I have learned to use these urges as red flags. If I resist the urge to escape and instead grab my thought wheel, there is always, always, always an uncomfortable feeling sitting right there that I need to explore.

The first step is to name the feeling.

Often, this is easier said than done. That's why I love *The Feelings Wheel*. It was developed by the late Dr. Gloria Willcox in 1982. In the example, you can see how helpful it can be to scan through the different words and see which one names the emotion you're experiencing precisely. I find it very helpful to move back and forth from the interior to the exterior of the wheel.

I may be feeling annoyed. Looking at the wheel, I see that "annoyed" falls under anger, so I ask myself, "What am I angry about here?"

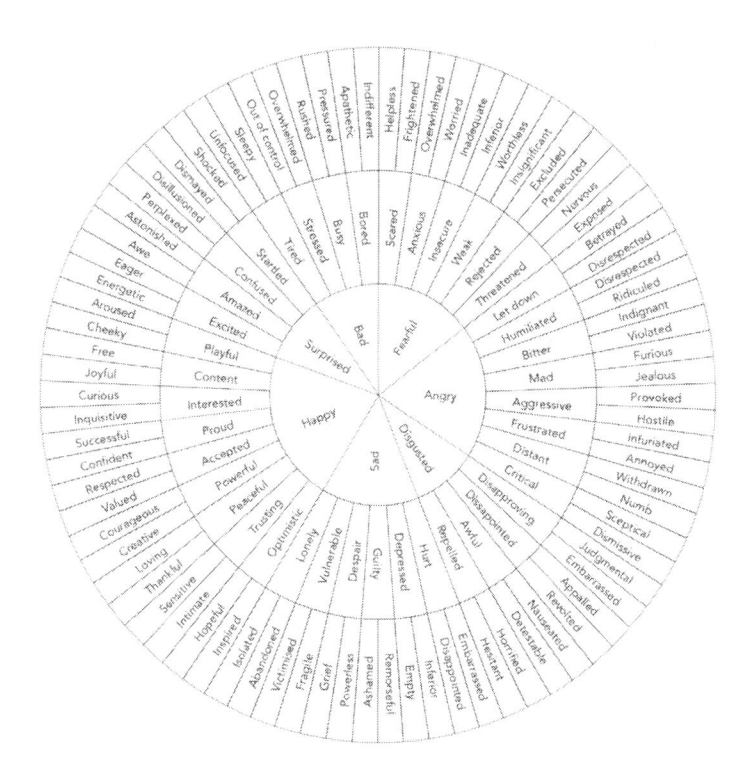

The Feelings Wheel was created by Dr. Gloria Wilcox

Putting the Two Together

One night I was scrolling Instagram before bed when I suddenly set the phone down and walked to the freezer. I paused. With my hand on the handle of the freezer, I said, "I think I need to grab my thought wheel instead of ice cream."

I genuinely didn't know what was pulling me to the kitchen.

I sat down and looked at the Feelings Wheel. I asked myself the Thought Wheel prompts, these are the answers I wrote that night.

How am I feeling?

Jealous. And sad.

What is the event causing this feeling?

I was scrolling Instagram and saw a mom post a photo of her daughter, who is similar in age to mine, at the beach smiling. The mom captioned the image, "We only get 18 summers with them."

What is the thought behind the feeling?

I am a bad mom. This is my only summer with my kids when they are ages seven and two. I haven't made any fun memories with them. My daughter LOVES the beach. We are halfway through summer, live in Florida, and I haven't taken her. She also loves the pool and keeps asking to swim, but I haven't taken her swimming. My son is obsessed with fish, and I haven't taken him fishing. I haven't done a single fun thing with my kids this summer.

What is fact?

- My daughter hasn't gone to the beach this summer. My son hasn't been fishing. They haven't been swimming. My daughter is seven. My son is two.

What are your thoughts about this fact?

- I am a bad mom. Good moms create fun experiences for their kids.

Which isn't true, I am a great mom. The reason we haven't been is because I'm bending over backwards, trying to get to the root cause of a health issue for one of my children, and it's taking all my energy to get through each day. I feel so stretched. I know that this is the highest priority for my family right now.

What is in my control?

- I can put plans on the calendar to do what matters to me.

What is not in my control?

- What other people are doing with their summers. Whether people say yes or no to joining me in the plans I will make.

Is there a new thought I can create?

- I am an awesome mom.

What can I learn about myself?

- I didn't realize how important it was to me to create these memories this summer. [Tears were rolling down my cheeks by this point.]

Are there any actions I can take?

- I opened Facebook Messenger and sent a message to my dad asking when he may be available to take the kids fishing. I sent a message to a friend and asked if she wanted to get the girls together to swim. I sent a message to another friend with kids who loves the beach. I asked her if she wanted to get a date on the calendar for us to take the kids together.

Within fifteen minutes, they had all seen the messages, and I had dates on the calendar.

If I had grabbed the ice cream instead of my Thought Wheel, none of that would have happened. I went to bed feeling like a weight had been lifted off my shoulders. I had taken my power back. I had reminded myself of what I could control.

Foreboding Joy

As you begin to practice using your feelings to tap into your thoughts, I want to warn you that it's not only our negative feelings we run from.

Dr. Gay Hendricks transformed my world with his book *The Big Leap*[2], which I cannot recommend highly enough. He talks about how joy is the emotion we feel most uncomfortable holding. For different reasons that he breaks down, we each have a glass ceiling we set for ourselves and how much joy we believe we are worthy of experiencing. When we begin to exceed that self-imposed ceiling, we will often self-sabotage.

Dr. Brene Brown writes[3] about this concept and explains it as joy being the most vulnerable emotion we can feel.

A gift you can give to yourself is to start noticing and holding onto your joy. Name it. Feel it. Claim more of it. Soak in it. Pursue it. You are worthy of abundant joy, and the more comfortable you become holding onto it, the closer you will get to releasing your favorite self.

If you feel the self-sabotage coming on, grab your Thought Wheel and Feelings Wheel. Reflect on why you may be holding yourself back. Give yourself permission to expand to places you have never gone.

Mental Health

It's important to me that we clarify the importance of working with a mental health professional when needed. There are many things we can coach ourselves out of or work with a coach to help us expand, but other things need to be left to the licensed professionals.

Personally, I have benefited from two types of therapy: talk therapy and EMDR, Eye Movement Desensitization and Reprocessing. I recommend clients to therapists as needed, especially for processing trauma, abuse, addiction, eating disorders, or challenging relationship dynamics.

In my own family, we have benefited from psychiatric care. I worked with a mental health professional to discover I have ADHD. I openly share that I take stimulant medication because I think it's important to reduce the stigma. Before my diagnosis, I was self-medicating with stimulants such as five servings of caffeine a day and sugar hits with every meal and snack. Understanding how my brain works, what it needs, and getting proper treatment has transformed my life. However, I wish the second D in ADHD didn't stand for "disorder." I have come to realize that the way my brain works is my superpower. Understanding how to meet its needs and avoid its kryptonite has been one of the most empowering experiences of my life.

Similarly, we worked with the Amen Clinics to get SPECT scans of my daughter's brain. They are a psychiatric practice that uses a holistic approach, and we were able to learn how to regulate her anxiety with food, supplements, and lifestyle changes.

I have referred clients to different professionals for depression, suicidal ideation, trauma, and other scenarios. For these reasons, I couldn't in good conscience write a chapter on growing your mind spoke and not acknowledge that sometimes it's more than just reframing your mindset - and that's okay. Investing in your brain will give you a better return than anything else you could spend your time and money on.

A.N.T.

The acronym A.N.T. stands for Automatic Negative Thoughts. Dr. Daniel Amen, a leading psychiatrist and brain expert, teaches this acronym to understand that your brain will always default to the negative. The "A.N.T.'s" that enter our minds are not in our control, but whether we choose to listen to and believe them is.

It's important to understand this concept because it allows us to separate our thoughts from our beliefs. Just because we think something doesn't make it true.

A common example of an A.N.T. is when you have a void of information. The human brain usually defaults to the negative when it finds a gap in knowledge. Have you ever texted someone and they don't get back to you quickly, so your brain starts making up information about why? Maybe something bad happened to them. Maybe they are mad at me. Are they missing? Has there been a car accident? The most common scenario is that their phone died, they're not looking at their phone right now, they saw the text but couldn't reply at the moment and have now forgotten to circle back, or some other simple explanation. However, our brains usually have to be trained to override the negative to make up a new thought that is more helpful.

We are not our thoughts. We are the beings that observe our thoughts. The sooner we can understand the amount of power that is in this statement, the sooner we can take ownership of our lives.

Decluttering the Mind

Many of us are walking around with thoughts constantly swirling in our minds. We can be sitting in silence yet drowning in the noise between our ears.

There are many tools that can help us to reduce this noise. Because these tools could fill an entire book by themselves, we cannot cover them in depth.

In my online courses, I explain more of the "how" behind each of these ideas, but here are some ideas to get you started on reducing the mental clutter:

Exercise: It's debatably the most beneficial medicine for your mental health. I am more motivated to get my workout in because of how much clearer I can think and focus than I am concerned about the appearance of my body.

Walking by yourself: Many people enjoy silence, a podcast, their favorite playlist, music with no lyrics, an audiobook, or just the sound of nature.

Journaling: This is one of the most powerful tools you can use. When we write, we not only connect our left and right brain, but we also connect our conscious with our subconscious. You may surprise yourself with what comes up when you begin journaling.

Task Management Systems: If all the tasks in your life live in your brain, you will feel overwhelmed. Regularly get your thoughts and tasks out of your mind and onto paper. Transfer them to appointments in your calendar so your brain knows when they will get done. The growth is then becoming someone who honors their calendar.

Meditation: There are many forms of meditation, not just sitting with your legs crossed and your elbows on your knees. I recommend exploring different guided meditations as a great place to start.

Sleep: Your mind will always function best when you are well-rested. Full stop.

Alcohol: Brain fog is a real thing, and alcohol increases it. If it's a daily or frequent habit in your life, try going longer stretches without it and see if your mental clarity increases.

Rituals: Create morning and evening rituals that incorporate many of your daily habits. This will free up the decision fatigue of having to actively think about these as to-do list tasks. A ritual becomes so ingrained that it's effortless.

The Mental Load of Motherhood and the CEO

Working with many mothers (or those in the primary parent role) and business owners, I have found that they carry a disproportionate amount of the mental load for their families and organizations. While everyone else just worries about their own lives, most mothers and business owners are mentally weighed down by thinking about ALL. THE. THINGS.

In most households, moms are the keeper of all the information. From what size clothes everyone currently wears, to managing every gift for every holiday and birthday party, moms' brains are overwhelmed with all the details. What needs to happen before kids can be out the door in the morning? What is still left between now and bedtime? Where are the missing items? Are we out of ketchup? Mom! Mom? MOM!! Hey mom. Where's mom? In most households with children, the mom is carrying everything in her mind.

It's very similar at work for certain roles, especially for small businesses owners who wear every hat. From how the company will make payroll, to stressing over the new marketing strategy, to figuring out how to fix the broken printer, there is no shortage of problems the brain needs to solve.

Researcher Dr. Marcus Raichle in his study, *Appraising the Brain's Energy Budget*[4], wrote, "In the average adult human, the brain represents about 2% of the body weight. Remarkably, despite its relatively small size, the brain accounts for about 20% of the oxygen and, hence, calories consumed by the body."

It's no wonder that we can feel physically exhausted after having to use a lot of brain power. Those thoughts are burning calories. There are a couple of ways I have found that we can reduce this mental load:

Do Less: Whether it's in business or family, oftentimes, we are asking too much of ourselves as a single human. Minimizing what is on our plate is a great first step. Much like my example from the self-care spoke about charcuterie and oatmeal dinners, sometimes the answer to having a smaller mental load is to simply lower our expectations of what we can do.

Share the Load: If you have a partner or older children at home, employees at work, or anyone running the show with you, take everything that you carry in your mind and put it onto paper. Let them see everything you are balancing and discuss how the load can be more evenly distributed. If you have the financial means to hire help, do it.

Create Rituals: Anything that needs to be done daily or weekly should be made into a habit and be known by everyone involved. Post these rituals publicly for all to see.

The publicly posted mental load and shared rituals have been transformational for my own mental health and for many of my clients. In the app, I share an example of the ones I use for my household and some context to the process I use to determine them.

Meet Maggie

Maggie's story is the tale of so many teenagers trying to navigate the modern world of adolescence. There was already pressure on kids to perform academically and in extracurricular events, but the addition of social media has created an intensity of social pressures that is causing an epidemic of anxiety in our youth.

Maggie's mom was concerned about the pressure her daughter was placing on herself, so she asked me if I would be willing to coach her. For the first twelve weeks of coaching, we rarely discussed any content outside of the mind spoke.

Bit by bit, we chipped away at why she had the thoughts she did, separated facts from feelings, and learned to use the Thought Wheel.

At one point, she started journaling each time she felt the emotion of anxiousness as a physical response in her body. We watched for patterns and trends of what was creating the most stress, and we were able to trace it back to beliefs about herself, others, and the stories she attached to those beliefs.

Maggie's tendency to feel anxious has decreased. She now describes herself as feeling free. Multiple family members have remarked on how much lighter she seems to be after a few months of coaching.

Maggie is one of many clients I have worked with who has found that their anxious thoughts have either greatly decreased or become non-existent. The common denominator among these clients is that they have learned to take control of their thoughts. By learning to acknowledge and ignore the A.N.T.s, focus on what they can control, and choose thoughts that will serve them, they can experience peace of mind.

Meet Monica

After working together for about four months, Monica sent me a text message that said, "My overall feeling of anxiousness that was pretty damn non-stop has gone away. I don't wake up every morning or go to bed every night with a weight on my shoulders and constant anxious thoughts in my mind."

Monica came to me as a working mom with two young kids and a husband who worked long hours each week because he owned his own business. She wanted a higher quality of life and knew something had to change. She had a dream to launch her own business but needed help laying a strong foundation.

We began with self-care work so that she could learn how to stop "shoulding" all over herself and create some healthy boundaries, then we moved into managing the mind. The Thought Wheel has helped her become aware of the made-up stories in her mind that weren't serving her. Now, if she's going to make up a story about the future that is unknown, she chooses to rewrite the fears with a positive prediction since she recognizes it's all made up anyway.

Monica has also used the displayed ritual lists to empower her kids to get themselves ready each morning. Now there is significantly less nagging around the house and they don't expect her to be managing their routines.

Quick Tip

If you choose to try the displayed ritual lists in your home, it's important to understand that I am not implying you tape it up and the work is done. You are shifting into the role of manager. You will still need to be the driver. The benefit is that by steering them to the lists and clearly communicating what you are holding them accountable to, you are not trying to manage all those tasks in your head. You are eliminating some of the mental load and clutter.

Affirmations

The first time I did a wheel, I didn't score well in the mental spoke because many of my thoughts didn't serve me. I spent years trying to lose weight, get stronger, and stick to "clean eating," but underneath all of that was hurtful inner dialogue. I didn't love my body. I was filled with shame about what I saw in the mirror. I was trying to punish my way into health, and it was never going to work.

It was quite an epiphany to recognize that my health goals were stagnant because of the thoughts in my mind. The first thing I did to address my thoughts was realize I needed to love my body as is. I took a piece of paper and wrote "I am beautiful" on it. I taped it to my bathroom mirror and recited it to myself, either aloud or in my thoughts, until I believed it. It took about six months.

When I first started, I felt ridiculous and like I was lying to myself. As time went on, however, I started to wonder if it could possibly be true. Several months later, I started to like what I saw. I started to believe I had a beautiful body. I had not grown any muscle or lost an ounce of fat. My body was the same, but the reflection was different. Until I believed I had a body worth loving and caring for, I was never going to attain the physical health goals I was setting. For me, the game changer was making my dialogue in the mirror a daily habit. The simple act of taping a piece of paper to the wall and assuring yourself of your worth can change your entire perspective of yourself.

When clients run a Thought Wheel and discover a new thought that can serve them better, I will often recommend they post it somewhere they will see it regularly. My bathroom wall has been covered in affirmations over the last decade as I am always working to write a new belief somewhere in my life.

What's Next

Visit the Mind Spoke pages in the journal to find some exercises that will help you work through this content yourself. As mentioned, this chapter also has many resources on the website with pdfs and videos that will help you take this work to the next level and apply it to your unique circumstances.

Chapter Five:

BODY

We are diving into the body spoke next because it's interconnected with the self-care and mind spokes. These three spokes go hand-in-hand because one new habit can serve all three areas.

My backstory

For most of my life, my subconscious belief was that the purpose of my body was to be admired by others. When I looked in the mirror, I wanted to see something that resembled the cover of the ESPN Swimsuit edition, but I was never remotely close to having that figure. As a result, the mirror became a place to have self-deprecating thoughts of myself.

I was an average-sized kid, but something happened in third grade that changed my perception of my body. I went from looking just like everyone else to being the fattest kid in my class. It was around that time other kids started making comments about my body.

I remember one time a neighborhood kid said something about me being fat, which I had never given any thought to at that point. A boy jumped to my defense and said, "She's just big-boned. It probably runs in her family. She's probably really strong and has lots of muscles." It was the first time I had considered the idea that I wasn't the same as everyone else. Why were they discussing my body?

My grandmother, my hero growing up, started to say I was so fat that you couldn't tell if I was standing up or sitting down because I was so round. Those later elementary school years were my first exposure to people having thoughts and comments about my body. As I progressed into middle school and high school, society, media, and cultural norms made it quite clear what the beauty standards were. I came of age at the height of the Britney Spears, Christina Aguilera, and Victoria's Secret craze. The message I internalized was: "Being desirable means you have to have blonde hair, a flat stomach, big boobs, and a gap between your thighs."

One day in high school, I remember watching two of my classmates take out a ruler and compare how much space was between their legs. My thighs have rubbed against each other since my third-grade growth spurt.

Thankfully, I survived those years, maintaining a fairly high level of confidence. I give full credit to my mother. Mom always had a special skill of building up our confidence. At my fifth-grade banquet, she insisted, "You were the prettiest girl there."

I rolled my eyes in a fifth-grade girl dramatic way, but a little voice in the back of my mind wondered, "Was I?"

When it was time to go back-to-school shopping for my first day of sixth grade, I didn't fit into any of the clothes in the kid's or junior's section, so my mom had to take me shopping in the women's section of the department store. She pumped up Liz Claiborne like it was the most high-end brand in the mall. I know she spent more than my parents' budget could afford when she bought my entire wardrobe from that section. My mom talked the associate's ear off about how cool Liz Claiborne was when she was growing up and how she just could not believe that I was going to get to wear that brand at eleven years old. Just unbelievable.

I remember walking through the halls of my new middle school in blue shorts and a thick yellow sleeveless shirt with stripes. In retrospect, it's how forty-five-year-old professional women dressed to go to the yacht club for lunch, but I didn't know better. When my clothes looked different than all the other girls, I thought it was because they were better and fancier. You can 100% credit my mom's parenting for that confidence.

Unfortunately, that couldn't protect me from the insecurities. I was unable to shop at *The Limited Too* like all the girls in my class because I couldn't fit in their sizes. I remember once walking to the field at P.E., and a boy called me a "fat bitch" because I was walking too slow. I couldn't help but notice I was different from all the other kids around me, and unfortunately, it came at the time when I was creating my personal identity and discovering who I was in the world.

When puberty hit in the eighth grade, my body changed again. I could start shopping at the stores in the mall like my friends, but the insecurities didn't fade. In high school, I was a size 10/12, while most of my friends were size 0. Once, during my senior year of biology, I got a D on a test.

As I looked at my score, I warped a story into my mind that the reason I got that grade was because I was fat. In retrospect, I can see that there is no correlation, but to my teenage brain my body was the reason for everything about my life I didn't like.

Being fat was the reason I believed boys didn't have crushes on me. The summer after graduation, I was hanging out with a guy friend and asked him why the boys didn't like me all four years. He said, "Oh, it was never about whether you were pretty. You are. It's that you're pretty intense. You're strong, know exactly what you want, and don't put up with any bullshit. That's intimidating to a teenage boy. We're conditioned to think our job is to ride in on a white horse and rescue damsels in distress. You didn't need anything. Teenage boys are just too immature to appreciate a strong female."

Being fat was an internalized belief I held about myself. It became the reason I didn't achieve any goals that I set my mind on. It was etched into stone, effecting the relationship I had with my body for decades, which I am STILL unlearning.

Diet Culture

I did my first trendy diet at sixteen. It was the Atkins diet, and I lost fifteen pounds, only to gain thirty pounds when I went back to a normal way of life. Over the next eighteen years, too many of my thoughts centered around what food was going into my mouth and either celebrating or shaming those decisions daily.

I share these experiences with you because I know that a vast majority of women, and many men, can relate to body shaming on some level.

BODY

I'm not interested in the conversations around who is to blame. There are many writers out there right now trying to determine whether we blame the media, a patriarchal society, the way generations of women have normalized how we talk about ourselves, or some other cause. For some, knowing where to point the finger allows them to be an activist in cultivating cultural changes. For me, it's not where I like to spend my energy. I am much more interested in taking my power back, discovering thoughts that serve me, restoring my relationship with my body and then passing on these new thoughts to my children, my friends, and anyone else who wants new life breathed into them.

We cannot shame our bodies into health.

We cannot hate our figures into a new shape.

We cannot guilt eat our way into pleasure.

However -

We CAN respect our bodies into health.

We CAN love our figures for the shape they are.

We CAN eat foods that bring us pleasure.

Speaking of *guilty pleasures*, can we please remove that phrase from our vocabulary? It's just a pleasure. Enjoy it. Or don't.

If it's harming you, then call it something else - maybe a vice. We are allowed to have pleasure for the sole purpose of joy. Pleasure is not a sin. It's fully living the human experience.

Let us begin with loving our bodies first. This is where the work starts.

Goal Setting

For about ten years, I set annual goals. Every year, I had one goal that made it onto my vision board: "Weigh 150 pounds by December."

Somewhere, somehow, probably due to the outdated system of the BMI chart, I determined 150 was the number that reflected whether this 5′ 7″ body was healthy or not. I achieved it twice in my adulthood and held onto it for a mere number of days because the habits that got me there were so utterly unsustainable. Years later, I learned the term *orthorexia*, "a condition in which somebody is very concerned about eating only foods they believe to be healthy, in a way that is not reasonable," as defined by the Oxford Dictionary.

In retrospect, I was struggling with an undiagnosed eating disorder for five years. On the outside, I looked like someone who was very concerned about healthy living, clean ingredients, and being well. But on the inside, I was suffering from an unhealthy obsession with everything I ate to the point that I could not fully enjoy normal life experiences.

On the tenth January that I set my 150-pound goal again, I finally had the epiphany that *maybe this goal isn't serving me*. Maybe being healthy wasn't about getting better at goal setting, habits, food, and exercise. Maybe I had health all wrong.

That year, I went on a journey to figure out how I even wanted to measure my health. A basic rule of goal setting requires it to be measurable, but I knew the scale wasn't cutting it for me.

I threw the scale away.

Yes, in the actual trash can.

And my mental health has never been better.

I have no metric by which to punish or reward myself. In the past, every experience on the scale led to emotional eating. I would end up with sugar after the scale, regardless of the number. If it went down, I would have earned a treat. If it went up, I felt defeated and wandered to the kitchen for a serotonin boost.

I no longer consider food by how it will affect the scale. Now I ask myself, "How will this make me feel?"

Some foods give me energy. Some make me tired. Some bring me joy. Some give me gas or brain fog, cause an allergic reaction in my eyes and on my skin, or flare up my sinuses. The ones that bother me probably won't bother you, so I can no longer label foods as "good" or "bad." In our house, the language is centered around how our individual bodies respond to that food.

So, if the scale couldn't be my metric, and I wanted to set a health goal, what metric would I use?

The Body Wheel

When I reflect on whether I am healthy, I now look at all the factors pictured here in my Body Wheel. I created this wheel as a visual representation of each of the areas of health I manage in my life.

You can be thin and be severely depressed and suicidal.

This is not healthy.

You can be thin and not realize your neck is out of alignment, which may cause you to suffer severe migraines.

This is not healthy.

You can compete in bodybuilding contests but have no flexibility, which can lead to easily injuring yourself.

This is not healthy.

You can be thin and be totally sleep-deprived. Your brain will not function well. It also increases your chances of issues later in life, such as dementia[5].

This is not healthy.

You can be thin, but your hormones are totally out of balance, so you are constantly frustrated with yourself, exhausted, snapping at your family, and experiencing a long list of symptoms in your body.

This is not healthy.

We can keep going.

The bottom line is that being thin does not equal health. Full stop. Your weight is ONE component of many to consider when evaluating your health.

So, where did I land on setting a goal for my health after the 150 had to go? For the last two years, I have been working with a doctor who measures over a dozen blood panels. We discovered I had a lot to work on. My thyroid and iron levels were all out of whack, so we started with balancing those. My hormones showed I was making too much cortisol (the stress hormone), so we balanced that as well. I was diagnosed with ADHD, and we have been treating and monitoring it with great success through prescription medication, supplements, and lifestyle changes. My health goal was to improve my lab results. I wanted to be told, "Great job. Keep doing what you're doing" by my doctor. I recently achieved it, so I am now focused on maintenance and seeing if I can improve my numbers to get off one of my prescriptions. This year, my body is craving to get stronger and more flexible. My goal is to listen to my body and honor her requests. Not only do I have more energy, more clarity, and a healthier self-image, but I also have so much more joy. I have taken five trips since I threw away the scale. For the first time in my adulthood, there is no way to punish myself when I get home. Have you ever done this? Have seven days of bliss and then come home, step on the scale, see the number went up, and immediately start beating yourself up about the salty foods and sugary desserts you consumed?

I'm learning to just soak in joy. To relish in the pleasures. To expand my capacity for more joy. My vacation diet and my day-to-day diet look almost identical. I mostly eat things the earth grows that give me lots of energy, but I say yes to the things that bring me joy, like tiramisu and ice cream with my kids. It's neither perfection nor ignorance. It's just life.

It's been the most freeing experience to watch my body transform with the help of my doctor and yet I have absolutely no idea how much weight I have lost. I dropped two clothing sizes and then my body stabilized. But the actual number I weigh…I have no idea. When I went into the office for a checkup a year after not seeing my weight, I stood backward on the scale and asked the woman to please not share the number with me. I'm self-aware enough to know that whatever number I would have seen that day, my brain would have quickly attached stories and meaning to the figure and re-inserted it as a measuring stick to my healthiness.

I've been able to enjoy feeling great, grow my Body Wheel areas and yet have not given energy to what affect my actions will have on a scale. I question how my choices will make me feel. What effect will they have on my brain and my energy? The results have been life-changing.

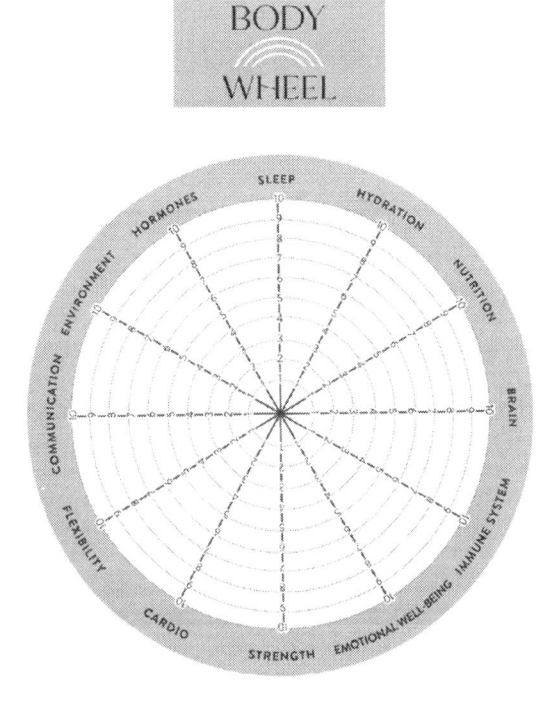

BODY WHEEL

- SLEEP
- HYDRATION
- NUTRITION
- BRAIN
- IMMUNE SYSTEM
- EMOTIONAL WELL-BEING
- STRENGTH
- CARDIO
- FLEXIBILITY
- COMMUNICATION
- ENVIRONMENT
- HORMONES

Here is a short description of what I am looking at when I measure each of these health spokes:

Sleep: The total sleep quality, which includes the length of time asleep, the length of time in deep sleep, and how well my body moves through sleep cycles. There are many ways to measure this. I personally use an Apple watch and the app AutoSleep.

Hydration: Total water intake. I have a goal of 100 ounces a day, but everyone's body is different. I pay attention to my energy levels, chapped lips, headaches, and urine color to show me if I'm staying well hydrated.

Nutrition: Tracking whether the food I am consuming is meeting my body's needs. Learning to listen to my body has been a better teacher for this spoke than any specific food plan.

Brain: Brain health is very important to body health. The more I have studied what my brain needs to be at its peak, the better my overall health has improved. Our mental health can be greatly impacted by our diets and lifestyle, so it's important to look at the physical components of our minds.

Immune System: A healthy immune system drastically improves your quality of life. In addition to sleep, water, and exercise, limiting the number of inflammatory foods I allow in my body and supporting my body with the right vitamins and supplements has helped me tremendously in this area.

Emotional Well-Being: Managing our emotions well allows them to move through our body instead of storing up inside us. This would also apply to healing trauma from your past that your body may still be storing.

Exercise: *(I separate strength, cardio, and flexibility into three different spokes because I want to make sure I am being intentional in all three areas. Having just one exercise spoke would make it easier for me to neglect a key area)*

Strength: This spoke is measuring the muscle growth and strength in our bodies which, positively enhances our metabolism, energy levels, and prevents injury.

Cardio: The benefits of cardio exercise are long, even if it's as simple as walking every day.

Flexibility: Stretching or yoga exercises are hugely supportive of the body. It is especially helpful in supporting your joints, blood flow, and preventing injury. I mostly love it for how it makes me feel in my body.

Communication: This was a very difficult spoke to name, but it's so incredibly powerful. From the brain down to the spine and throughout the nerve endings, our body sends messages. Our energy is also moving and flowing through us and can get blocked as well. Whether it's chiropractic care, massage, acupuncture, energy work, or other fields, there are many ways to support the ability of the body to communicate with itself.

Environment: This spoke measures the environments in which we live. Whether it's mold in a house, pollution in the air, or fragrances from a candle that cause headaches, there are many environmental components that affect our bodies.

Hormones: Having properly balanced hormonal levels can significantly improve the body. It's so important to work with a professional in this area because age and gender play a huge role in what is appropriate for one person versus another.

Budget-Friendly Beginnings

As I write about my experience, I am fully aware that not everyone has the same access to healthcare or the discretionary income to invest in professional help in some of the areas mentioned. Please know there is still a tremendous amount you can do to improve your health in the meantime.

Regarding food choices, look for registered dietitians who are putting great content out into the world. Between social media and podcasts, you can start overcoming diet culture myths by shifting where you get your advice. The only protocol system I ever recommend to people is to use the elimination diet for a short period of time to explore how certain foods affect their bodies. In our family, we have discovered multiple food sensitivities and allergies this way. It's not a weight loss plan or something that is meant to be a way of life but rather a valuable personal experiment.

Sleep and water intake are two of the most powerful, transformative areas we can focus on. I cannot stress this enough. My husband and I track our sleep nightly. When we first started monitoring our total sleep and our deep sleep, it was fascinating. We chose to make it a top priority in our family and have rearranged our lifestyle to accommodate everyone in our house sleeping well, including my husband and I sleeping in separate bedrooms. Some might think this decision is strange, but we chose to make sleep a higher priority in our family than what others think of us.

Water is just as important in our world. We each have our own water bottles we carry around, and we track our intake. Even my eight-year-old daughter carries a 54oz bottle to school every day and finishes it. She can feel the difference between when she has enough water and when she does not. She will often be moodier, have low energy or get a headache if she hasn't had enough that day. In the same vein, if you are not getting enough rest or enough sleep, your body cannot run all its systems at its best.

Eating healthy has gotten a bad rap for being expensive, but I have found that potatoes, rice, bananas, and beans are very economically friendly and can be the base for many healthy options. I also recommend making one change at a time. Just make one meal healthier to start. You don't have to change all your habits at once. Look for something good you can add in and replace something you're willing to let go of.

Exercise doesn't have to include a gym membership. Going on walks at a nearby park is beneficial for cardio and mental health. YouTube is filled with at-home fitness workouts as well.

After learning how to meditate, I firmly believe that if it were a pill people could buy at the drugstore, most people would have it in their cabinet. The effects of deep breathing and learning to manage our thoughts can be life-changing in our bodies. The emotions we feel all get absorbed into our bodies. For example, heart attacks are well known to be associated with stress. For this reason, I included an introduction to meditation as a free resource in my app.

When I was pregnant, my hips started hurting. The chiropractor and midwives told me this was because my body was adjusting to prepare for childbirth. After the baby was born, they still hurt. They told me it was natural. My body was recovering from childbirth. By the time she was six months old, the pain in my hips was so excruciating that exercise and sex became painful. Fortunately, I crossed paths with a Jin Shin Jyutsu practitioner, also referred to as Japanese acupressure. He cleared all the pain in one 90-minute session. Pain that I had been tolerating for a year by that point. The place in my hips where the pain was intense were the energy centers for joy. Through that session, I realized that I had not allowed myself to experience joy for a year, despite my first child being born. We were under tremendous financial stress and life change. My body internalized it all as guilt.

When I was caring for my child, I felt guilty that I wasn't working my business to bring in more money. When I was working, I felt guilty that I wasn't giving my child attention. When I was playing with her, I felt guilty that I wasn't cleaning. Our home was in a constant state of mess. When I was cleaning, working, or caring for my child, I felt guilty that I was almost entirely neglecting my marriage. We were in survival mode, and my body felt it all as guilt, which stored itself in my hips. That evening on that practitioners table I was meditating while he was doing his techniques. I envisioned all the guilt leaving my body. He taught me a technique of where to apply pressure if the pain returns. All these years later, I still return to release those centers sometimes.

Since then, I have eliminated most of the guilt by focusing on staying present. I work hard to redirect my thoughts to the experience in front of me. I block proper time for all the priorities in my life. When I am with my kids, I try not to think about work. I have my set hours and if work pops into my mind, I remind my brain that we will get to that when the time returns. When I am at work, I don't worry about my kids. I know they are safe and loved. I pour myself into the task at hand. I schedule time for my husband, my health, the chores, and anything else I am juggling. This allows me to stay present where I am.

Learning to manage our emotions and our minds can have healing effects on the body. I highly recommend the book *Burnout: The Secret to Unlocking the Stress Cycle* by the Nagoski sisters on this topic.

Overeating

Most likely, someone is reading this and thinking, "That's all fine and dandy, Sophia, but I know that I need to lose fifty pounds to be healthy, and I'm aware that my overeating habits are what need to change."

If this is you, try this exercise. Buy a journal and write down your plan for your food each day, including portions. You can plan it out once a week or once a day. Just make sure each morning you are going into the day with a written plan of what you will eat.

Then, journal what you ate.

Do they match?

When they don't, learn from that.

Was it a lack of preparation and intention? Were you still hungry and need to add more food to your plan?

Was this about emotion or compulsion? If so, each time that urge comes on or you want to reflect on why it had power over you, run a Thought

Wheel (Chapter 4). For many people, the answer to their overeating rests in finding new tools to help them feel their feelings. Oftentimes, our brains don't want to feel uncomfortable emotions, so a nice dopamine or serotonin hit from certain foods will offer a wanted distraction.

Emotions like loneliness, guilt, sadness, discontentment, and many more can lead to emotional eating.

For most of my adulthood, I didn't know how to listen to my stomach and my hunger cues. My brain, and its compulsion to use food to feel better, dominated my relationship with food. For me, being able to quiet my mind was also linked to being able to stop at "enough" versus being stuffed.

If this goes on for a while and you cannot self-manage your way out of it, I highly recommend therapy or a coach. There are fantastic tools to help you navigate this world. You don't need to do it alone.

Your Why

If you have a desire to make significant changes to your health, I recommend beginning with a strong "why." Answer the question: "Why does this matter?"

The answer to that question becomes your motivating factor. It also becomes the split-second thought in your mind when you have to decide. Knowing what's on the line matters.

I have a short-term and a long-term *why*. Short term, I want to have high energy and a clear mind so that I have the capacity to take care of myself, my family, and my clients well. Long term, my why is that I want to live a high quality of life into my 80s. I want to be 82, teaching a yoga class and wearing out the youngsters. Taking care of my body now is how I get there.

Meet Shane

Shane came to me with a clear *why*. He has diabetes, and his doctor explained that he is still at a point where he can get off the medicine and reverse this, but he has to follow through with the recommended lifestyle changes. After making no progress for a couple of years, he hired me to help hold him accountable and offer new tools to achieve this goal.

He already has a successful business, a great family and many of his life goals accomplished. But what's the point of all of that if he doesn't have his health to enjoy it? The side effects of the medicine he takes are lowering the quality of life he wants to live. He wants off them. He is making tremendous progress because his *why* is so clear.

The tools that are working best for him are the ones I mentioned. We began by journaling the food plan and results. This revealed some gaps to me, so I referred him to a registered dietician who helped him learn how to re-incorporate carbs into his life and build a food plan that was sustainable long term instead of trying to expect perfectionism.

We also used the questions in the Thought Wheel to discover the correlations between thoughts, feelings, and food choices. Shane was able to realize that managing the thoughts that were leading to the most stress in his life was a significant solution to him avoiding those late-night unhealthy snacks most of us have experienced.

In just a few months, Shane made tremendous gains in his physical health after years of struggle. Ditching the diet culture messages, finding sustainable practices, paying attention to how foods make him feel, and managing his thoughts and habits were the game changers. The same is true for almost all of us.

What's Next?

Twelve areas of health can be intimidating if you have several that need work. Remember that you are playing the long game here. This is not about a 30-day or 90-day quick fix. This is a lifetime journey.

My recommendation is to identify ONE habit you want to focus on first. Put all your intention around that habit. Go all in until you find a sustainable practice that feels like a permanent life change and not a sprint. Then, pick the next one.

To keep your life simple, consider starting with some habits that will overflow to many areas. For example, prioritizing my morning walk checks so many boxes all at once. On my Body Wheel, it improves my cardio, brain, emotional well-being, and sleep (exercise can improve sleep quality). I started walking a track that has outdoor exercise equipment to help my strength training. I will sometimes add a short yoga flow with meditation at the end of my walk. I drink water before and after. That one practice each morning now improves almost every single spoke on my Body Wheel. The icing on the cake is that if we pop back over to the *Favorite Life Wheel*, it also helps my self-care and mind spokes. That walk is also one of the best things I can do for my brain. I can think more clearly and focus better after my walk. The self-care benefits of going out into nature, by myself, with my thoughts, offer benefits for me for the rest of the day.

This wheel will always ebb and flow. It's a dance. The goal is not perfection but growth. The Body Wheel is my lens of how I look at my health, but you have to reflect on what is your own lens. How will you measure the progress in your body spoke? What does "being healthy" mean to you?

In the journal, I offer a version of the Body Wheel where you can write in your own spokes in case your lens looks different than mine. You are also welcome to replicate mine if it serves you.

At the end of the day, the most important question to ask yourself is, "What does my body need from me right now?"

Visit the journal pages to reflect on your best next steps.

Chapter Six:

SPIRITUAL

Spirituality. Oof. This word can bring up a mixture of emotions in a crowd.

For some, this word has connotations of peacefulness and rest.

For others, this word feels like a punch in the gut and brings up complex feelings ranging from pain to uncertainty and many experiences in between.

Let's all take a deep breath together and know that everyone is safe for the purposes of this conversation. Because this is a discussion about your favorite self, you get to bring all of you to this chapter. There is no agenda of how you should show up here or how any of these questions should be answered.

For some of you, your religion is an integral part of how you will interpret these questions and how you will form your answers. Please bring your faith with you. It's an important piece of how you move through the world.

For others, religion has no place in your spiritual experience. You will find these questions just as relevant and helpful.

I want to offer a warning for the content of this chapter. I know many people who have experienced spiritual trauma. I will be sharing my personal journey in the pages ahead. It will include some Christian church-related experiences, and I will be sharing some scripture references as well. I'm discussing those topics because I am opening up parts of myself, my story, and my experiences to let you see inside my world. This is not to influence what values you choose for yourself, but rather to offer my experience of figuring out my own.

For those who may read that paragraph and think, "What? People are so sensitive nowadays that this author is offering a freaking trigger warning because she quotes the Bible. What has this world come to?" I am going to ask you to lean into curiosity here. Ask yourself the question, "Why would she feel it necessary to write that?"

The reality is many people have had very traumatic, abusive experiences in their lives in which people have used Christianity, God, and the Bible to cause them great harm. Their pain is real. Spiritual trauma is a heavy burden to carry. Because I don't get to know the past experiences of the readers of this book, nor can I fully know how raw their wounds may be or where they are on their journey to healing, it is an act of kindness to let them know what they are walking into. It allows them the option to skip to the next chapter for their mental health should they need to.

For the purposes of this work, let's define spirituality as your alignment with your purpose values, and being connected to something larger than yourself.

Are you living your life with intention? Do you know your purpose, right now? Do you know the legacy you want to leave behind? Do you have clearly defined values? Are you living in alignment with those values? Do you know your why, your motivations, and your deepest fears?

The spiritual spoke is where we do the work of diving into these existential life questions.

Whether you are familiar with this type of work or have never given it any consideration, I believe you will find value in this chapter.

Who are you?

To answer these questions, you must begin by figuring out who you are. This is probably the hardest work you will ever have to do.

Most of us are walking around with definitions of ourselves that other people have handed us. Maybe it was your culture, family system, the media, religion, marketing companies, education, or a role model that shaped who you believe you "should" be. Discovering your true identity and releasing the one you have been conforming to most of your life is a liberating experience.

It was Socrates who said, "To know thyself is the beginning of wisdom," some 2500 years ago. Humanity has been wrestling with this idea for a long, long time.

If you want to unleash your favorite self, you must first define your favorite self.

For me, this experience began in 2011.

When My Journey Began

In February 2011, I was sitting in church when I had an out-of-body experience. I cannot even tell you what the pastor was preaching on that day. I just remember an intense feeling overcame me. I became aware of a woman who was inside of me, and it felt like she was calling out to me.

It was quite a juxtaposition. I had an awareness of her deep down inside of me, longing to be born. Simultaneously, I could feel a higher self calling for me to reach up and grab her hand so she could lift me out of the water to breathe.

Something came over me. I started grabbing every piece of paper I could find. Using golf pencils on the back of tithing envelopes, I started writing down the words that were coming to me like a vision. It felt like someone else was writing through me.

This woman, who felt so foreign at the time, described herself as calm. She meditated daily. She took care of her body and mind. She was generous. She was mature. She was wise. She was financially wealthy. She was a leader and a teacher.

This vision was so far removed from who I was at that time. I was twenty-four, deep into hustle culture, and never took time for rest or self-care. My normal rhythm was to push through difficulty, suppress my feelings and pain, and sacrifice my needs for the benefit of work or others until I couldn't take it anymore. Every three to four months, I would take a bubble bath, let all the tears out while the water ran, go to bed early, and then start the cycle all over again. I was stuck in a hamster wheel, never moving forward but exhausting myself, nonetheless. I was drowning in debt that kept growing, didn't have the intimacy with my partner I wanted, and wasn't prioritizing myself or my family.

I don't have a better language to describe what came next other than to say I felt God telling me I needed to take a sabbatical. I had never even used the word sabbatical before. My heart was racing, and my gut had fallen to my toes. I knew with certainty I had never known before that I needed to spend a week by myself in silence. My life was too busy. Too noisy. I was always on the go. I needed to force myself to sit in my home and get very quiet, so I could understand what to do next.

The Sabbatical Experience

It took me a week to rearrange plans and commitments to clear my calendar. I asked my husband to go stay with friends and take the three cats with him. I was working an independent contractor job at the time, so I was able to set my own schedule and take time off.

Four days after my epiphany in church, I had a major work event with over 500 people, including most of my clients. I was supposed to be hosting and working the room, but my body started visibly shutting down. Shortly after the doors opened, my boss looked at me and sent me home. I crashed into bed and was sick for days.

It could have been worse. There are many stories of people running their bodies into the ground and ending up in the hospital. This was just exhaustion. I've seen it in many other people since. They spend most of their vacations in bed because as soon as their body gets a hint that it has a chance to recover, it shuts down.

When I woke up Friday, I was alone and secluded for the first of nine days. I figured it was time to start trying this meditation thing. I did the legs crossed on a pillow posture, but that felt stupid after about two minutes. My thoughts bounced everywhere.

Next, I dusted off my big yellow book with the black letters I had purchased at Barnes and Noble but never opened, *Meditation for Dummies*. I scanned through it only to get absolutely nowhere. It felt like a foreign language.

In the depths of my soul, I knew I needed to figure this out. I had spent my most formative years praying to God in a way that was all me talking, ranting, venting, and asking. I kept a prayer journal so that when people asked for prayer requests, I could write them down. When I would sit down to pray, it sounded like a little girl on Santa's lap: "Please fix this," "I want this," "Please help this person with this."

My gut knew this wasn't it. This wasn't what the scriptures talked about. This wasn't how it was supposed to work.

The church had taught me how to talk to God, but I didn't know how to listen. How do I sit in silence and HEAR God? What does it really mean to "be still?" I resonated with the disciples who fell asleep when Jesus asked them to pray all night.

I was frustrated. I was alone.

Having no idea what I was going to do for nine more days, I opened my laptop. I had intended to have a device-free sabbatical, but I needed help.

I remembered hearing that one of my old college professors, Dr. Bagley, had recently retired. He was one of the professors I would stalk during his office hours to see how much one-on-one time I could get to pick his brain. I remembered that one time he mentioned beginning every morning with a 30-minute meditation. I reached out to him on Facebook to see if I could ask him some questions about how to meditate.

That was Friday at 9:29p.m. Several days would pass before I would see a reply.

In the meantime, I deep-cleaned and organized our 470-square-foot studio condo. I purged old files, almost catching the house on fire when I decided to burn them in a pot on the back porch, and then tried finishing them off in the oven. I practiced using all the settings on my camera. I'd started a photography business before learning how to shoot using manual settings. I'm a jump- and-figure-it-out-on-the-way-down kind of gal.

In retrospect, my undiagnosed ADHD is on full display in this story.

On Wednesday, my professor replied.

Unconditional Love

Before I share with you what happened on that day, I first want to rewind a few years and share with you a pivotal moment when Dr. Bagley changed my life in college.

He taught Advertising 101. However, he would open every single class with something philosophical. It was usually a Rumi poem, but sometimes a parable from Jesus or a Chinese proverb or something from a Hindu or

Buddhist tradition. I was very confused about his ideology, and most of what he shared went over my head. I am a naturally curious person, so I found him fascinating and perplexing, but most of the students thought he was kooky and wasting their time with weird stuff.

But one day, he walked into the class looking disheveled. He was clearly disturbed. His face was filled with sorrow.

In his hands, he held the stack of graded papers from a recent test we had taken.

He looked at our class and explained with deep grief in his voice that in this stack of papers, he had to give two students zeroes. He had caught two people cheating while we were taking the test, and for ethical and academic reasons, he had to assign a consequence to the action. And then I will never forget what he said next.

With tears rolling down his cheeks, he said, "However, I need you to know that this does not change how much I love you. When I look at my classroom filled with students, I do not see faces. I never see faces. I see beauty." Choking on each word and with tears leaking down his cheeks, he continued, "Every time I walk into a classroom, I see beautiful souls worthy of nothing but love. And if you believe that this effects how I see you, I need you to know it absolutely does not."

Woah.

You could hear a pin drop.

None of us knew how to respond to this moment.

At that point in time, I was twenty years old. I had been in Baptist churches since I was ten and was in the middle of helping plant a new church. This would have been circa 2007 and the rise of the trendy "pastors in blue jeans" movement.

At this moment, all I could think was, "This is what Jesus was talking about. This is what unconditional love looks like. This is what it means to be free of judgment and full of love. This man is more like Jesus than any person I've ever met in church, and I don't even know if he is a Christian?"

Something in me broke open that day.

I couldn't make it make sense.

Why have I spent ten years showing up to church three times a week, surrounded by Christian leaders, mentors and teachers, yet I've never seen a love like this displayed?

How do I see the beauty in every person like him? I want to live like that.

How do I become so free of judgment that when someone wrongs me, I am more concerned with them knowing they are still deeply loved?

I loved me some Jesus. I devoured the scriptures from a young age. I wanted to live in the ways he taught. The sermon on the mount wrecked me every time I read it and still does to this day.

That moment was the most Jesus-like story I had witnessed, and it took an out-of-church setting to encounter it.

This was the moment that the first card, the one at the tippy top, was removed from my fragile house of cards.

Thursday Came

My piddling around the house continued for a few days. On Wednesday, Dr. Bagley replied and answered my meditation questions. Our back-and-forth messages led to him extending an invitation to come to his home.

I drove forty-five minutes to his house that Thursday morning and sat on a chair in his living room. I had so, so many questions.

I was desperate to wrap my mind around this concept of meditation and listening to God. How does one do it?

What I didn't know was that I was opening Pandora's box. I spent my youth living in black and white. In early adulthood, there began to be many gray areas. This conversation would become the key that opened me up to a stunning world of color. I would never be the same again.

It began logistically. I wanted to wrap my mind around what happens after he closes his eyes. What is he thinking? Does he do that leg-crossed thing? How does he not fall asleep?

He explained that every morning he reflects on his values and sits on each word. He listens to what comes up. If he is living out of integrity with any of his values, this is the space where he often realizes it and can reflect on the experience.

He explained that reconciling his values with his actions is where most of his growth comes from. These quiet morning hours were always where he realized his shortcomings, his opportunities to extend more love, more grace, and more forgiveness.

He told me the story of how meditation carried him through the time when his child he had known as his daughter for a couple of decades transitioned to becoming his son. He shared with me the intimate moments of navigating that as a parent. I'll never forget when he said that through these meditations and regularly recentering on his values, what began as an intense, emotional experience he believed was about his child turned out to be about his need to expand and grow. He learned through reflection that it was not about influencing his child but rather about expanding into the person who could be the unconditionally loving parent his son needed.

Keep in mind, as I write this in 2022, these conversations are much more common and public. In 2011, when we spoke, this was so rare to hear about and even more so when he and his family were navigating through it many years before that.

This was my first encounter with someone in the trans community's story. It had always been something confusing and distant until that moment. He openly answered my curious mind's questions. His son was now an ordained minister and full-time employed clergy.

Obviously, this was exploding a lot of barriers in my mind.

This part of the story makes me think of the quote Ted Lasso made famous, "Be curious, not judgmental." It is my predisposition to move that way through the world. I was born with an insatiable curiosity. In the fourth grade, I remember my teacher, Ms. Blakemore, nicknamed me "question girl" because, after almost every concept she taught, I would raise my hand and ask follow-up questions, the most common one being, "But why?"

During that conversation, what would have happened if I had chosen judgment? A transgender man is a professional clergy. In our world right now, many people who claim Christianity as their faith are losing their minds over such ideas. All I wanted to know at that moment was how to live like he did that day in the classroom with the students who cheated.

Our conversations turned to me asking him how he lives free of judgment. I still had many judgements I was clinging strongly to. He became deeply curious about what I felt were black-and-white, right-or-wrongs in the world.

I remember one by one listing them off, and each time, he asked me how I would respond in unique circumstances. For example, we would all agree that murder is wrong. However, we justify it when it's to kill someone who is murdering others. We justify a parent killing someone to protect their children.

The deeper we went, the more and more gray things became. Many truths we cling tightly to are true until their exception arises.

If love is a river flowing freely, judgment is one of the quickest ways to build a dam, often with just a few words.

We can all agree that it's wrong to intentionally cause harm to others, and consequences follow accordingly. No different than the students who received zeroes on their tests. But in what circumstances do we remove our love for the other person?

More than a decade later, I am still wrestling with this idea.

How do I choose love despite the pain I feel? How do I see the beauty in all people even when their actions are so detrimental? How do I live in a way that I am a walking example of the forgiveness Jesus spoke of? That there is no end to the number of times I forgive?

This is the work.

As our conversation continued that day, he had errands to run. Rather than me getting in my car and leaving, he invited me to tag along. While he picked up items for dinner from Fresh Market, I tagged along, asking more and more questions.

Eventually, we landed on purpose. He asked me what mine was. I had no idea.

He shared with me his personal experience of how he found his.

He was at a seminar, and the facilitator provided index cards. He was instructed to fill each card with a single role he plays in his life and what he loves doing. At the time, he was a professional in the advertising and marketing industry. The cards were filled with words like husband, father, reader, friend, and such.

They were then asked to lie on the ground and hold the cards to their chest. Then, one by one, imagine having to let go of that role/interest for the rest of their lives. They could continue living their lives, but this thing would no longer be a part of their experience.

At first, it's easy. But then you get down to the last handful. Could you continue living if you were no longer a father, husband, or friend?

He told me that he laid on the floor with the last few cards in his grip. With tears, he imagined how he could continue going on without his family. But the last card, the role he couldn't let go of, was the one where he had written "teacher."

Following that experience, he left his career, moved states with his wife and children to enroll in a PhD program, spent a few years in near poverty to get through school, and was later able to begin his career as a professor.

I am so grateful to say that after that very thought-provoking day, we stayed in touch. He agreed to be a mentor to me. For the next two years, I drove over about once a month to continue having my many questions answered. And by answered, let's be clear, I don't think he ever answered them like a dictionary can provide clarity and specificity. He mostly asked me questions in return and provided a net to catch me in love as my house of cards kept crumbling down.

Coming Home

Leaving his house that day, I decided to drive to, of all places, Ikea. I was hungry, and the vegetable soup from their cafeteria sounded just right.

I remember walking around in a bit of a daze, sitting on different sofas and reflecting on the hours of dialogue we had just had.

With the last couple days of my sabbatical, I wanted to bring clarity to my life's purpose.

When I got home, I tried the purpose activity. Since I didn't have any index cards, I just took a notebook and wrote each role down on one line.

When I reflected on what I was doing when I felt the most alive, I couldn't help but visualize the hours and hours and hours of conversations with friends. Whether it was in a coffee shop or on a walk, I yearned for deep dialogue around growth, expansion, chasing dreams, and figuring out how to overcome obstacles. In an attempt to put a name to what role I was filling in these life-giving conversations, I wrote, "Helping others grow."

One by one, I ran a line through every role in my life. Wife, daughter, sister, photographer, advertising account manager, friend, etc.

All I knew was that I could overcome any loss in my life, no matter how great, if I could keep engaging in conversations centered around helping people dream, believe in themselves, and execute.

At the time, I had some friends who kept a vision board in their kitchen. I had never read any books about them or why people made them, I just thought it was a cool concept to look at your goals each day.

I turned the page in my notebook and asked myself the question, "If I died today, what would I be disappointed never happened?"

Some of my responses were predictable, but others were quite surprising. I wanted to pierce my nose. I wanted to help my little sister plan her wedding. At the time, she didn't even have a boyfriend. I wanted to see Key West, backpack through Europe with my husband, and have a flat stomach (hopefully, you've read the body spoke chapter and realized that's changed).

The item on my board that was the hardest to reckon with was my yearning. The dream that was so important to me, so tender, so raw, that to even allow others to know it felt much too vulnerable.

The truth was, I longed to help others grow, but not just a small number. My heart longed for significant impact.

I found an image of a developing flower. Four stems at different heights. Underneath, I wrote, "Full-time job helping enrich others' lives." Then, on each stem, I wrote "Blog. Videos. Speaker. Life Coach."

One thing was quite clear to me, though. I had a hell of a lot to figure out before I could teach anyone anything. My life was a hot mess.

What Next

My sabbatical and the Thursday I spent with my professor were in the middle of a very long spiritual journey. I had been on this road for many years. There is a decade more of that journey, mostly filled with pain and obstacles, which followed that encounter.

If you are familiar with Joseph Campbell's *Hero's Journey** concept, my experience sitting in the church would be my catalyst, which sprung me into an opportunity to meet a guide.

For my lens of how to view the world, I turned to Galatians[6] in the Bible. There is a letter Paul wrote to some growing churches.

In Chapter 5, he criticizes them for getting too caught up in the laws. They were too concerned with who was and wasn't following the rules.

He says, "The only thing that counts is faith expressing itself through love."

The whole chapter is beautiful. It's amazing how relevant it still is nearly 2,000 years later. Humanity really hasn't changed. This is my favorite part of ancient texts. To see that their struggles were no different than ours are now.

This chapter is most famous for what's been coined, "the fruits of the spirit." Paul goes on to say, "But the fruit of the Spirit is love, joy, peace, forbearance [patience], kindness, goodness, faithfulness, gentleness and self-control."

My dad likes to say, "People get so caught up on the fruits of the spirit because they are warm and fuzzy, but they forget to pay attention to the verse before that - the acts of the flesh."

Paul also warned, "The acts of the flesh are obvious: sexual immorality, impurity and debauchery, idolatry and witchcraft, hatred, discord, jealousy, fits of rage, selfish ambition, dissensions, factions and envy, drunkenness, orgies and the like." *

---

*If you're not familiar with the Hero's Journey, Google it and click on images. It's a framework for how good stories, like movies, are told. The protagonist must hit each of these points in the story.[1]

I decided this would be my guide. Rather than concern myself with who called themselves a "Christian" or who used the correct vocabulary words, I would just use these characteristics as a magnet. When people's lives reflected the fruits of the spirit, I would lean in and get curious. I would move toward them, wanting to hear their story. Understand their path.

When their lives reflected the acts of the flesh, I would just step away. They are on their own journey, but they don't need to be a leader I follow.

This was what led to the pile of cards on the table. My loss of clarity and identity. My house of cards had crumbled.

The more I dove into the American church, the more I came face to face with hatred, selfish ambition, and dissension. The hardest thing for me to reconcile was that the church was where I learned judgment. There is a constant fear spread through the culture that we need to be "in the world, but not of the world." There is a deep sense of us versus them. Either they are one of us, or they are of the world and therefore suspicious. Invest in relationships only with the intent to convert. Dissension was rampant as leaders sought to declare which denominations were "one of us" or not.

I encountered plenty of kind people who had fruits of the spirit in the church. What I couldn't rectify in my mind, was why the people I found filled with the deepest and widest amounts of those fruits often were not. If we are all Children of God, and the light is in all of us, why can't I learn from their light too? I couldn't get behind the belief that they didn't also have wisdom to offer.

The more people I met, the more opportunities I had to travel the world, and the more time I spent with people in my backyard who looked different than me, the more these barriers didn't work.

After releasing the framework, which I been following since I was ten, I had to discover what would be my new tools. Tuning into my desire to listen and meditate, I wanted to start there. Just get quiet. Using the lessons from Dr. Bagley, I decided to start by reflecting on my values each day. For the first time in my life, I asked, "What are my values?" I had always been told what my values were by others. I decided the values I would meditate on were the fruits of the spirit. Whenever I would meditate, I would just sit and breathe in and out, reflecting on those words and my actions. I added two other words that were important to me: gratitude and authenticity.

The pursuit of living my values led me closer to God but away from the church. The first three years that followed leaving the church were filled with intense loneliness and pain. Everything about my identity and community was gone.

I titled my work *Unleash Your Favorite Self* because I want everyone to experience this freedom. I have learned that before you can unleash yourself, you must release yourself. In other words, something must break to create a path for something else to step forward. But this chapter right here, this releasing I am sharing with you, nothing has been more painful in my life than shedding the faith I was handed and setting out on a journey to find my own. When we use the word unleash, we may think of a caged bird being set free. At first, it looks beautiful, watching the bird soar through the air. But in reality, unleashing also comes with so much hardship. To unleash anything in our lives means to leave something else. It means to completely leave behind a known comfort and discover how to survive in the wilderness. Whether someone is leaving a bad marriage, a miserable job, a toxic friendship, or anything else, it's normal for it to be one of the hardest seasons of their lives.

The hardest part of the church is what it's purposefully built around, "We are a community that believes the same things."

I wanted to live in my integrity and part of that was not hiding who I was. I couldn't keep sitting in pews and chairs pretending I agreed with some of the groupthink when I knew I didn't. I wasn't okay with the fact that a transgender friend wouldn't be welcome to be themselves in this environment. The more I realized we all have so much more in common than separates us, the more my skin would crawl hearing people focused on those who are different.

If you have ever experienced a faith transition of any kind, I see you. I know it's so hard. It wasn't until I felt like I could stand on solid ground again that I realized the entire experience was plagued with grief. Loss of your identity. Loss of community when you no longer fit in anymore. Loss of intimate relationships. Loss of friendships. For many people, it can include the loss of family members if they don't respond well to your change. My relationship with my family never felt the same after I was the only one to leave the church.

I want to encourage you if you are reading this while in the middle of a faith transition. You can find wholeness again. Your range of emotions are absolutely okay. The pain will birth an incredible sense of freedom as you move through it. And lastly, I recommend moving your attention toward what you do want rather than focusing behind you on what you don't. Follow where you feel the warmth. Follow where you feel life, not death. There is no right place to land, just what's right for you.

Healing My Spiritual Spoke

Let's circle back to Chapter 2, the *Favorite Life Wheel*. This was how the wheel changed me.

I only knew what I was running away from. I hadn't done the work of figuring out what I wanted to run toward. My spiritual spoke was so low. I felt so alone.

From about 2012 to 2016, I was the only person I knew who still intensely loved the Jesus story and was actively wanting to grow closer to God but couldn't step foot in a church without extreme discomfort.

How do you find community?

The wheel revealed to me that my lowest spoke was the spiritual one, and it wasn't an option to keep running away and avoiding. It was holding me back everywhere else. I had shed an old identity, and it was time to find a new one.

Years after my experiences, I heard the language deconstruction and reconstruction. It perfectly described what I was going through before Instagram and TikTok were talking about it. My house of cards fell, and I needed to build a new home out of different materials.

The first habit I adopted that helped me improve my spiritual spoke was listening to podcasts. I typed in the name of a former pastor, Rob Bell, who wrote many books I loved. He was publicly shamed out of the church after he started asking questions that you aren't supposed to ask and challenging some of the sacred cow ideas. It turns out that after disappearing from the limelight, he had been releasing a weekly podcast for over a year. I binged every episode over a couple of months.

One night, while washing dishes and listening to an episode, I fell to my knees in tears. No one had ever described my pain so clearly. He described precisely what it feels like to be spiritually homeless, lose your community, and feel completely alone. He put language to emotions I didn't know how to describe and then let me know I wasn't alone. That there were thousands of us, and everything was going to be okay. He told a parable that described my experience and ended with returning to peace and clarity. For the first time in years, I felt a sense of hope. Maybe I could find community again. Maybe I could feel grounded again.

As one may expect, this was hard on my parents. I will never forget a specific moment in my kitchen. It was 2018, two years after that "washing dishes" moment. I hadn't been in church for about four years and was going through a really, really, really hard time. My mother started crying and summoned all the courage in her to bravely say to me, "Sophia, I know you are mad at the church. I know you don't want to go anymore. But God has been laying this message on me that I'm supposed to tell you it's time to go back. And you don't have to come to mine, but to go somewhere."

At the time, I was carrying many stressors, but the heaviest at that moment was that I was at the end of my second pregnancy, which had been very physically challenging for me. On top of the issues causing me intense physical pain, my son was breech and was supposed to have flipped six weeks prior. If he didn't, I would be going in for a c-section in a few days. I was planning a home birth, so it wasn't quite the experience I had anticipated.

I use the word brave to describe my mom's comment because I have an extremely assertive personality and had made it very clear to my family that I was done with church. I was also very pregnant, hormonal, in a lot of pain, stressed at work, and my husband was traveling for work almost the entire pregnancy. She knew fully well that those words could cause a range of emotional reactions from me and that she was taking a risk.

I responded to my mom saying, "Actually, there's a church I've been following online and am really curious to check out. But they meet at Eleanora's bedtime (My daughter was born in 2014), so I haven't been able to go. If you keep her for me, I will go this Sunday."

I drove thirty miles down the interstate. They met in a venue that, during the weekdays, operates a café with a mission. The café is a social enterprise that employs people who were formerly homeless, addicted, or incarcerated. Some employees are provided safe housing, which serves as a bridge to stability.

I pulled into the parking lot and saw Mercedes and BMWs parked next to twenty-year-old Toyotas. I walked into that service knowing no one and found a seat. The walls were covered in art by local artists. When the music began, a Black transgender woman had a microphone and was singing with the rest of the worship team. I later found out she was living in transitional housing despite coming from an affluent family because, unfortunately, the statistics are too true that their ability to be themselves in the world is plagued with obstacles.

After the music, the pastor led everyone through a guided meditation. Rather than avoiding politics and controversial subjects, he leaned right into them. He told the story of the Black female journalist who ended up converting a member of the KKK because she chose to confront him with kindness and invested in a relationship with someone she knew hated her. His sermon connected the intentions of Jesus' message and life with our modern-day problems.

I looked around the room and saw demographics that reflected America. There were elderly couples, young families, so many different skin colors, sexual orientations, and people dressed like they probably had a lot of money next to someone dressed like they were probably homeless.

At the end of the service, I watched the transgender woman leave holding hands with her partner. He was pregnant. And in this room, he was also wrapped in love. I spoke with the pastor afterward. He shared with me how they were trying to help this couple get resources for their baby, along with the appropriate medical care. I also found out that the pastor had a transgender family member, had personally been through addiction recovery and was twenty-four years sober from alcohol. These factors said so much to me about his ability to lead people through pain, through love, and through overcoming. He understood the resurrection story of dying and being reborn at the level I wanted to engage.

I don't have words for how this experience helped to heal me. Peace overcame me that I didn't realize I had been searching for deeply. Prior to that moment, I had lost hope for the church. I didn't know if I could ever experience what Jesus had intended for his disciples to create.

During the pregnancy, I figured out how to feel my son's head. I know with certainty that he was still in a breach position that morning. While I was sitting in that service, I felt him move in a way that I didn't recognize. It was different. In my heart of hearts, I fully believe he turned while I was sitting there.

The next morning was my appointment with the O.B. They had already scheduled the surgery room at the hospital for me. I was going in on Thursday at 1:30p.m. for an attempted manual flip and labor induction. If it didn't work, they would perform a c-section. This appointment was the last ultrasound to confirm he was still breach and proceed with the plans.

When they scanned my uterus, my son was in the perfect laboring position. Not only had he flipped, but he was perfectly centered over the birth canal.

You can take whatever you want from this story. You may call it a coincidence. You may call it a miracle. Personally, I think it's connected to a tension I had been holding in my body for so many years that I fully relaxed when I sat in that room.

A peace had overcome me that I hadn't known in so long. My faith was restored that the church could actually look like Jesus had intended. That the love of God was big enough for everyone and it was possible for people to share life together who, at the surface, were so different but in reality, were so alike. My pain and grief I had carried for so long healed while I sat there and witnessed the kind of church I read about in the scriptures.

The Most Important Question

So, what does all this mean for you? This spoke is intimately unique to each individual. My journey to inner freedom is going to look quite different than most of yours. The journal will guide you as you reflect on many of these ideas and questions for yourself, but let's take a look at some of the most important questions.

At the top of this chapter, I said that the most important question to answer is, "Who are you?" Not who you think you're supposed to be.

If you can answer that question, then write it out. If you read that and think to yourself, "I have absolutely no clue," then don't stress over it. I invite you to begin exploring. What brings you joy? What makes you light up? What are you fascinated by? What are you deeply curious to understand more?

Deciding Your Values

Clarifying your values is so important. For years, I used the values I shared in this chapter. But then Brené Brown challenged me to pick a top two in her book *Dare to Lead*[7]. I chose love and authenticity. It was a game-changer. When you put values in order of priority, it will offer tremendous insight into how you navigate decisions in your life. What a phenomenal tool to walk through life, having clarity around your value system and what it means to live in integrity for you. It also offers great value to recognize that we are all walking around this earth with different values at the top of the list.

Consider what your top two values are. Are they different than those around you? When we go out into the world, we regularly share life with people who have different value systems than we do.

For example, different values often show up in financial decisions. Some people would rank fiscal conservatism as their number one value. I take huge financial risks regularly and don't need a lot of financial certainty to find peace. If the decision is made from love and authenticity to what I believe I am supposed to be doing in this world, I'll risk it all. But other people would find that risk unbearable. My decisions and their decisions will be very different, but neither is wrong. We are operating with different value priority orders. In the next chapter, we will dive deeper into this correlation.

What are your values? Which ranks in the top two? Looking inward and asking some of these really important questions will give you so much clarity on who you are, and where you want to go. Then you can begin answering the questions about how to get there according to your own integrity.

What do you want?

Most people are chasing what they think they are supposed to want. I want to challenge you to reflect on what you *actually* want.

As Neville Goddard coined, "What you desire, desires you."

I was first introduced to the concept of "begin with the end in mind" in the book *The E-Myth Revisited* by Michael Gerber[8]. He challenges the readers to envision their own funerals and what is being said about them by friends and family. This can be very similar to the exercise I mentioned the first time I made my vision board. If you died today, what would you be disappointed never happened?

I challenge my clients to write their own eulogies. The thought may sound morbid, but the clarity it offers you on what truly matters to you is profound. Filtering all your decisions through the lens of the legacy you want to intentionally create offers clarity that most people are lacking. In the journal, I offer many prompts for you to consider as you seek to answer these questions for yourself.

One of those questions is what is your purpose, right now? I added the "right now" because sometimes it changes with seasons or circumstances. You may gain value from the exercise that my professor shared with me. But do you know what? You may not. How we all look inward is different.

As you're looking for this answer, also try asking other questions like, what are you doing when you feel most alive? Last year, my therapist asked me that question. I paused, took a deep breath, and all I could see was myself teaching an audience. Whether it was five people or thousands, it didn't matter. When I asked my husband the same question, he answered, "Sitting around a fire pit with my people." Those answers brought tremendous clarity to both of us and helped us narrow down where to spend our energies.

This chapter is simply a woman's memoir if you stop here, but that's not where the most value is. The greatest value is in going over to the journal and doing this work for yourself. Who are you? What are your values and your purpose? What do you really want? Start there and see where it leads you.

Chapter Seven:
FINANCIAL

In college, I heard motivational speaker Rita Davenport at a conference. She was in her seventies and had been successful in business during a time in our history when women were breaking through the kind of glass ceilings I will never know. In her thick Southern Belle accent, she said, "Money isn't everything, but it's right up there with oxygen." I think of that quote often. It got a laugh from the audience, but it's also a somber reality.

Money is required for housing, food, transportation, healthcare, clothing, water, electricity, and other basic needs. If you are part of the population that has discretionary income after the basic needs are covered, money also buys access. It buys independence, experiences, therapy, coaching, conveniences, support systems, and so many other products and services. It's quite interesting to watch how people interact with this spoke. Some people begin from a place of fear. We often fear what we do not understand. Other people begin from a place of confidence. They can navigate this spoke with ease. Whether it's because of their knowledge and experience or because it comes naturally to them, this spoke is not as complicated for them to create the success they desire.

There is no debate that of all the spokes on the *Favorite Life Wheel*, this one is my greatest personal challenge. In the beginning, it was ignorance for not knowing better, but now it's about my free spirit. I do not like feeling boxed in, limited, or told I cannot have what I want. Add to that my ADHD and finances being detail-oriented. It's a constant growth process for me.

Thanks to the Enneagram, a personality typing system that I often incorporate in my coaching, I learned that one of my core fears is missing out on maximizing what life has to offer, and another core fear is looking at my pain. Well, apply that to finances, and you have someone who values experiences over a savings account and doesn't want to look at her budget when it's tight. When there's plenty of extra money, it's fun to drag and drop all those line items. When it's been a hard month, I battle the urge to just look away.

On the flip side, that may make me one of the most helpful people to write financial content. It makes me think about the relationship advice I've gotten from someone who has been married for fifty years versus the advice from someone who has been divorced. Both individuals have valuable perspectives. The married couple has five decades of wisdom and insight. The divorced friend can often share what went wrong and how they are applying those lessons the next time around. When it comes to finances, just know this is more like a conversation with a divorced friend.

My Mess

I started my first "big girl" job with a desk and a management title when I was eighteen, a few weeks before I started college. Therefore, I thought I was an adult and ready to be on my own.

A few months later, I got engaged. On the day he proposed, I was debt-free, and he had just a few thousand in student loans. Before we finished college four years later, our net worth was more than $150,000 in the red. We managed to purchase a condo the month the housing market peaked in 2006. We bought two new vehicles, one of which was my dream VW Beetle. I custom-ordered and drove her off the lot myself the day she arrived. We financed Brandon attending a private university with no scholarships. For anyone curious, yes, we had parents every step of the way discouraging every single one of these decisions. But we were stubborn and "grown-up."

Post-college, we decided the best way for him to pursue work in the film industry was to start a photography and cinematography business. We opened a business credit card when I was twenty-three. Within a year into our business, we managed to accumulate $25,000 in additional debt buying all the gear we needed.

For anyone who has ever ridden the waves of entrepreneurship, you know it's a rollercoaster. I remember we had our first $20,000 month when I was twenty-four, and I quit my job a couple of months later. But then there were $2,000 months, and we couldn't pay our bills. So naturally, the credit card debt grew.

By 2013, we were expecting our first child, living in a wildly upside down 470 square foot studio condo and drowning in debt. We burned ourselves out in the wedding industry by working every weekend. We took the gamble and both started different entrepreneurial journeys to try and supplement the gaps.

That year, we had to short sale our condo to get out from underneath it. We had accumulated so many monthly payments from all our debt that we couldn't even come up with the money to rent somewhere to live.

At seven months pregnant and in our late twenties, we had to humbly move ourselves back into my parents' house. We slept in my old bedroom. My brother's old room was now my mom's craft room. She moved everything to one half of the room, the other half was converted into the "nursery" where my expectant daughter's things would belong.

I remember one day when my sister-in-law mailed me an entire box of baby clothes she bought. I sat on the couch and cried tears of gratitude and shame. I couldn't afford to go to a store and buy a wardrobe for my child. How were we going to do this? I filled out the paperwork and got myself and the baby signed up for WIC because we qualified, and I knew I needed to be humble enough to accept whatever help we could get.

That season felt like rock bottom.

Climbing Out

My daughter was born in January 2014. By December 2019, we paid off the last of the student loans and were officially debt-free except for a mortgage. In those five years, we had purchased a home, had a strong foundation under us and were finally building up a healthy savings account.

The reality of how we got out was one painful lesson at a time. One step at a time. In full disclosure, we leveraged help from our support system. No one ever wrote a check to clean up our messes, but they gave us roofs over our heads, offered access to financing to help the cleanup process, let us borrow vehicles when ours were in the shop, and shared lots of wisdom when we were humble enough to realize we didn't know it all.

Over the course of those five years, we both grew our businesses and increased our income, but that wasn't what created the shifts.

The most powerful thing we did was learn how to live on a monthly budget. We shifted from spending money and then figuring out how to pay for it— to spending the money on paper and intentionally telling it where to go before it came in. In Chapter 2, I mentioned the power of using daily habits to change your life. This habit of syncing our budget daily was forcing us to look at the pain even when we didn't want to. It was absolutely the difference maker.

Seeing our budget daily, staying up close and personal with how much was coming in, and telling it where to go helped us become much more intentional about every decision we made. We also became more aware of how much it really took to run a household.

Eventually, we both took a few years to get jobs. We became W-2 employees and turned our businesses into side hustles while we climbed out. The pandemic forced my husband back into freelancing. We waited for me to take the leap until after our emergency fund was over three months of income and he was making enough to cover our basics. Thankfully, our net worth is now the inverse of its worst. Similar numbers, but in black, not red. We aren't ready for retirement; we can't stroke big checks for fancy toys yet, but we have done the most important work. We've created healthy habits to stand on that will take us toward all the financial goals we are pursuing.

The Big Picture

It's easy to get caught up in the weeds of logistic conversations like budgeting apps, investment options, insurance coverage, and the like. However, there are a million blogs, podcasts, and books that will break all of that down for you. I want to show you the foundation we use for all our decisions and how we interact with money now.

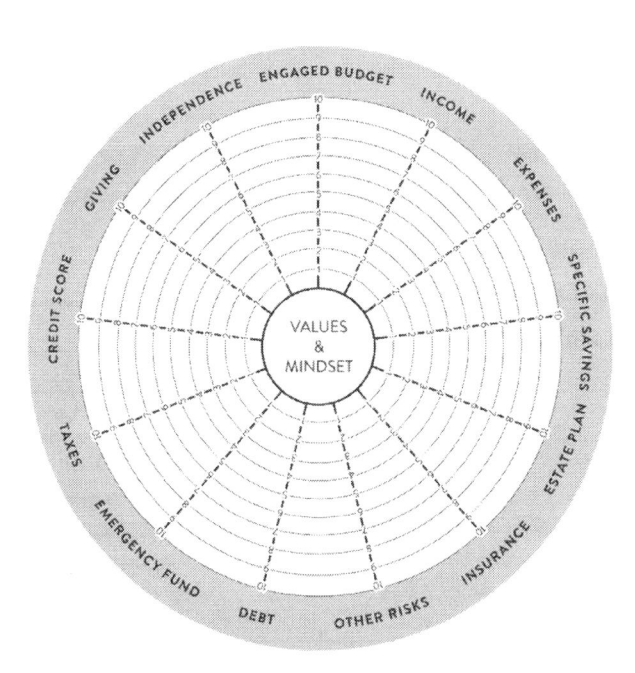

FINANCIAL WHEEL

Wheel sections (clockwise from top): Engaged Budget, Income, Expenses, Specific Savings, Estate Plan, Insurance, Other Risks, Debt, Emergency Fund, Taxes, Credit Score, Giving, Independence

Center: Values & Mindset

Have you figured out yet that I love wheels? Whenever you are looking at your life or zooming in on a specific area of it, wheels are such a great way to see things holistically. You have to look at all the moving parts of your life and how they interact. Finances are no different. Where you begin will always be different based on your circumstances.

However, one thing is different about this wheel from the others in this book. You will notice it has a center.

It is not by accident that I placed the spiritual spoke directly in front of the finances. Our purpose and values are central to how we interact with money in every facet.

Values

How we spend our money reflects what we value.

I've heard it said before that becoming wealthy doesn't change you, it reveals you. Generous people become philanthropists. Selfish people revel in their greed. Your values are at the core of your finances.

When you complete the work in the spiritual spoke of determining your values and prioritizing them, it will give you tremendous clarity over how you want to interact with money.

Knowing who you are and where you want to go are the fundamental questions that must be answered before you can create a financial plan for your future.

I have a friend who is living his dream. He moved to the mountains to live on a family farm with his mom, wife, and child. Their days are spent cultivating gardens and milking cows. The family combined their resources, sold their home in a large city, and bought a remote property to live their desired lifestyle. He creates an income online selling handmade products, his mom has a remote job, and they all contribute to caring for the land. At the core of all their decisions is their value in caring for the earth. In order to live in alignment with his personal integrity of a minimal footprint and caring for our environment, this move was the right choice for him. They are living a very minimalistic lifestyle, require a much smaller income than most, and are full of joy, peace, and contentment.

I have another friend who has built enormous wealth. Conversations with him regularly blow my mind. Around the age of forty, he got heavily involved in politics. If you really want to see him light up, ask him policy questions. I once asked him what motivated him. He said that he got a small taste of politics in his youth and quickly noticed that it was much easier to make a significant impact if one is financially independent. So, he put his blinders on and threw himself into business. He built up companies and sold them off until he had enough money to live the quality of life he wanted for his family. Then, he had both the margin of time and financial capital to be very effective in politics.

Fifteen years later, he could look back with tremendous pride at the projects and issues he had touched on and how much of a difference they had made for his community. I remember him beaming with pride when he said, "Every time I drive past that fire station, it is so fulfilling. Our community needed another one for so long, but the process to actually make it happen took me over ten years of determination to make it possible." He was also living his values and had created a life full of joy, peace, and contentment.

When you look at the drastic difference between these two value systems, it creates a completely different financial picture. Neither one is right nor wrong. One family is living off an average American family income, and the other is living a seven-figure lifestyle. When you look at the spokes on the financial wheel, the circumstances that would define a 1, 5, or 10 in each area are radically different for these two families.

Everyone's path is different. It's your responsibility to be in tune with yours. Even in these two examples, you can live in alignment with the value of caring for the earth while also generating a large income if a different lifestyle is right for you. There are also many examples of people who have had a tremendous impact in their communities through politics and didn't have to become wealthy first to do it. Your value system and how you define a 10 in each of these spokes will be as unique as you are.

This is why you must closely guard what advice you allow into your life. One person's recommendation on what you "should" be doing in an area can be far removed from what will actually help you unleash your favorite self. Most likely, when they give that advice, they will be projecting their fears and their values onto you.

I believe it's important that we remember this truth: we only judge other people for what we judge ourselves for. If you are very judgmental of people who have accumulated wealth, why? What underlying belief do you have about money? Could you actually have a deep, unmet desire to create your own wealth? If you are someone who is uncomfortable with money, I challenge you to reflect on this question: When I achieve my financial goals, how will my values shine through?

Mindset

Did you know that fear is responsible for holding millions of people back from their favorite financial life?

Many people walk around with a lens of scarcity. This means they hold a core belief that there is only so much money in the world, and they are trying to get their piece of the pie. They often make decisions from a belief that there is not enough or will not ever be enough. This attitude will show up in every financial spoke as fear gripping the steering wheel of their vehicle.

However, if you study economics or learn from those who have, you will find that the exact opposite is true. When many people have more, even more people have more. Abundance creates more abundance.

Money is not a limited resource. It's a resource that is in constant circulation. The more hands it passes through, the more there is to go around. Energy is a great metaphor for money. Think back to the self-care spoke. The more energy you store for yourself, the more you have to give to others. The more we get enough sleep, exercise, nourish our bodies, care for our souls, and manage our minds, the more everyone around us wins. The same is true for money.

Moving from the mindset of scarcity to abundance was one of the most powerful changes I made in my financial spoke. Once I understood that there was no benefit to living in a constantly broke mindset, I started correcting my thoughts and language around money.

A simple example of how I applied this in my life was when I stopped saying, "I cannot afford to _____." I changed it to, "Right now, I have higher priorities for where to spend my money."

I absolutely love travel, and there have been multiple times I had to sit out on girls' trips that friends were going on because there just wasn't the discretionary income. Previously, I would say, "I can't afford it." As I shifted my mindset around money, I would say to myself, "I can afford that. I have that money in the bank. But if I spent it there, I won't be able to pay for X, Y, or Z this month. I need to choose my priorities. When I have more income or fewer expenses, I'll be able to make that a priority." (The X, Y, or Z may be mortgage, food, daycare, gas, or any other financial goal). It helped me to feel in control of my money and not a victim of circumstances. It also gave me a sense of hope that as I continued toward my goals, there would come a time when I would be able to say yes to everything I wanted. Delayed gratification is healthier than constantly telling myself no.

As we discussed in the mental spoke, the way we feel has a powerful effect on how we interact in the world. Feeling broke, poor, or afraid of money will overflow into how we make financial decisions. Feeling hopeful, in control, and empowered will lead to better outcomes.

The Financial Spokes

Let's break down the financial wheel in more detail. Our values, mindset, and priorities are going to tie into every spoke, but most especially the first four listed below.

Independence: Financial independence is a point where your money is making its own money, and your time can be freed up for whatever you choose. Many people would label this spoke as retirement and use investment accounts to set long-term goals for their later years. However, I don't love that label here because many people are finding great joy in encore careers post-retirement, so they may never actually retire in the traditional sense of the word. In contrast, many people leverage real estate, specific business models, or invest to create financial independence much younger than the stereotypical retirement age. The bottom line is this, we all need a plan for how we'll financially be okay if we can no longer work, want to explore something different, or need to stop working to care for someone. Financial independence buys the freedom of choice.

Giving: Generosity is a core component of a healthy money mindset. Many people have different opinions on how much of your income should be set aside for giving and where it should go. This is going to tie directly back to your values and priorities.

When we were first married, we religiously gave the first 10% to the church. When we stopped attending, we began budgeting a monthly contribution to a "giveaway" line item. There are few greater feelings in life than when you feel far away from "being wealthy," but you have stored up quite a bit in that account and can stroke a sizable check to help someone.

I'll never forget the first time we were able to use this new giving model. Someone posted about a coworker who was a single mom of three kids and needed her car fixed, or she would lose her job. She couldn't drive to daycare or work. In 2014, I remember crying that I didn't have the $700+

to fix our Honda Civic. A few short years later, when I saw that post and checked the giving account that was growing each paycheck, we were able to pay a stranger's $800 car repair bill anonymously. We were making the average income for an American household. We weren't special or wealthy. We had just learned how to manage our money and choose our values.

Engaged Budget: Notice I was intentional in not just referring to this as the budget spoke. Many people have sat down and made a budget one time, only to never revisit it. They don't know where their money is going each month and aren't actively syncing the plans with the execution. The level at which you engage with your budget will impact every other spoke on your wheel.

Income: Simply put, this spoke reflects how much money is coming into your household. However, it's important that you align this with your values. Are you generating income in a way that allows you to live in your integrity? Does your income limit your ability to live your favorite life in either direction? Some people may love what they do, but that line of work might not provide enough of an income for them and their family. Other folks may stay in a job because of a high wage, but it's costing them their health and relationships because of stress with long hours. Do your income and values align?

Expenses: Your expenses are all the money going out. Do the line items in your budget reflect your values? Are there changes that need to be made for you to take care of your highest priorities?

Taxes: We are all affected by taxes in our budgets. Are you managing yours ethically? Is this area of your life neat and tidy, or is it a hot mess, stressful, or shady?

Emergency Fund: Emergencies are inevitable. I used to think unanticipated expenses were a disaster and so stressful. Then, I accepted they were part of life and just started planning for them. It's amazing how stress vanishes. Depending on which financial advice you listen to and how much risk is involved in your income stream, most experts recommend somewhere between three to twelve months of your income sitting in a savings account, easily accessible.

Specific Savings: This is separate from an emergency fund. When planning your finances, there may be different things to save for. You may need to save for a home down payment, a new car, college, vacations, house projects, or many other life expenses.

Debt: The amount of money you owe for purchases you financed. I live in a worldview that debt is neither evil or awesome. When used properly, it can leverage money to improve your life. When used poorly, it can create a disaster— as I shared in my story.

Other risks: Debt is a risk, but there are so many other parts of your life to consider here. Do you have a one or two-income household? How solid are those income streams? How many dependents do you support? Is your line of work dangerous or high profile? What other factors in your life affect your financial stability that should be considered?

Insurance: This spoke is intertwined with the risks and liabilities. There is a policy to cover you against almost everything. However, insurance eats up a tremendous amount of a family's budget, so it should be purchased wisely. If anyone is dependent on your income, do you have proper life insurance? That's the first place to start. Not having a proper home, health, or auto insurance can send families into bankruptcy when catastrophic events occur. I do not believe in using insurance as a form of an investment portfolio, but I do believe it's vital to work with professionals to get the right policies in place.

Estate Plan: There is nothing sexy or appealing about an estate plan, but it's a cornerstone of a good financial plan. If you do not have a will and other important documents in place when you pass, your entire life is turned over to the government to manage on your behalf, which creates major headaches for your loved ones.

Credit Score: Love it or hate it, it's a reality of the world we live in. Knowing your credit score, actively monitoring it, and keeping it high is going to make your life easier. Otherwise, if you ignore it until you need it, you may discover a disaster that takes time to be cleaned up.

What's Next

To get the most value out of this chapter, I recommend hopping over to the journal pages to assess where your financial wheel currently is and consider how your purpose, values, and mindset are showing up in each of these areas.

Chapter Eight:
CAREER

I wrestled a lot with keeping this spoke titled career. The word career automatically implies a paycheck is associated with your work, and that's not true for all people.

Modern culture has idealized the message that in order to maximize your life, you need to turn your purpose or passion into your career. Although I have done this for myself and have found it to absolutely be rewarding, I also fully recognize it's not the right path for everyone. I could say the same thing about having children, something idealized by culture and personally rewarding for myself but again, that doesn't mean it's right for every person.

It's also beautiful if your career right now is being a caretaker, maybe for your children or another loved one. Maybe you are retired and looking to create a new purpose in your life that isn't attached to finances. There are so many scenarios where someone's life can be filled with great purpose, and it doesn't involve an exchange of money for time or services.

I know so many people who live with the purpose of being a parent. Investing in the next generation is important work. There are many people who choose to work a job because it provides them with the lifestyle they want for their family, or their full-time job may be their family. This can be enough.

I see so many people burdened with the "should" of society that something in them may be wrong because they don't have the hunger, drive, and aspiration to accumulate career achievements. Just in case there is a reader who needs to hear this: Desiring a simple life is enough.

If your dream is to have contentment within your home, resources to provide for your family's needs, and the time to enjoy each other's company, that is enough. Write it down for the definition of your 10 in career and family on your *Favorite Life Wheel* and let go of any pressure or expectation implying you "should" want more.

In contrast, there are many people who find that this simply is not enough. They feel a calling from deep within that tells them their mission goes well beyond their microcosm. If that's you, I see you. I was born that way, too. My children bring me tremendous joy, are an incredible gift, and are a full-time responsibility, but my life's work transcends well beyond my household. I always knew my purpose and my career would collide. It was only a matter of how and when. If that resonates with you too, then when you define your 10, go as big as your dreams allow yourself to visualize today. And know as you achieve them, it's fine to expand that 10 to new levels.

Neither one of these life choices is right or wrong. Neither should be put on a pedestal or shamed. The only thing to glorify is a person having the guts to step outside of the "shoulds" and find their inner freedom to do what is best for them and their family.

I can also think of dozens of people I personally know who have had successful careers that provide them with the resources to contribute to their passions in the ways they desire. The first group of people who come to my mind is the volunteers at our local theater. My daughter got a small taste of theater at age eight and was interested, so when we found out our local community theater was putting on Charlotte's Web over the summer, she auditioned and was given a role.

The entire play was made possible by volunteers. The board, the director, the costume designers, the stage designers, the actors, and more. I am so grateful for all the amazing adults who shared their gifts and talents out of a place of pure joy to make this artwork come together for the community and our children. It didn't cost a dime for any of the children to participate. They introduced theater to my daughter, which not only made her come alive but pivoted her interests at a very influential age.

How was that possible? As I spoke with the people who were most responsible for this production coming together, it was obvious this was their passion and, for several of them, their purpose. Their love of theater and the arts lit their souls on fire. I learned through conversations with them, each one had a day job. Those jobs provided the resources for them to provide for their family's needs and have the margin in their lives to donate their spare time to the community.

There are many who would say, "To love theater with such a passion means you should find a way to do it for a living." It's important to me that we temper these comments with a "…well, maybe, but not always."

Personally, I think Elizabeth Gilbert[9] said it best. In her book *Big Magic*, she explained that she knew her purpose in life was to be a writer. She poured into her work with her entire soul, but she was hesitant to expect that her art would support her financially. For the first ten years she wrote, she never made a dime. Once she did start making money from her writing, she waited another ten years to allow it to support her fully financially, that was only because *Eat, Pray, Love* had become a bestseller. She shares her belief that expecting your creativity to fund your life can stifle that creativity. She found other jobs or income streams outside of writing until the time was right.

I share these stories with you because I once had a love of photography. Naturally, in the capitalistic culture I was raised in, it seemed like the obvious next thing was to make an income from this love. I spent seven years running a photography business. Although I am grateful for all the lessons I learned from it, I also mourn the loss of my joy in the art. Running a photography business is about 10% taking photos and 90% marketing, sales, accounting, editing, and every hat of owning a small business. I closed my business several years ago, and to this day, when I pick up a camera, it feels like it weighs 100 pounds.

This is where the spiritual chapter comes in so handy. If you haven't done those journal pages yet, then you'll miss some of the value this chapter has to offer.

Think back to the question, "What are you doing when you feel the most alive?" As I described already, my husband and I reflected on this question. When I got honest with myself, I found that I feel most alive when

I am speaking to an audience, but my husband said he feels most alive when sitting around a fire with family and friends.

In my world, my purpose and my paycheck naturally align. Helping others grow, teaching, speaking, and writing all align within a career that can make a living. And unlike photography, the work needed to run this kind of business does not burn me out.

For my husband, he's discovering in midlife that he is ready for a transition. After fifteen years of climbing the ladders of the film industry, he's realizing it's not an industry that can provide him what he truly wants. He craves routine, calmness, ample time with family and friends, and more peace. The film industry requires you to be ready to upend all your plans at a moment's notice. The hours, schedule, and project timelines are perpetual unknowns. In an effort to create the quality of life he desires, he's learning a new skill. He plans to pivot his career in the future. He sees his purpose as wrapped up in caring for his family, and the time away from them for the sake of the next project isn't as rewarding as it once was. For others, this pivot could be a grave mistake that would leave them filled with regret for the rest of their lives. For him, it's a death and a rebirth. You grieve the loss of what once was. But releasing it creates the freedom to design something brand new, which for him, involves a lot more time around the fire pit with some whiskey. Only you can know your own truth.

You may be like me and are able to attach these three things together: Your career, your source of income, and your purpose. This is beautiful and a gift. Everyone is worthy of it if it's their desire. The other ways of designing a life are just as beautiful, a gift, and everyone is worthy of them, too.

So far, we have identified three categories of how you may align with your career:

- Your career provides a paycheck to support your lifestyle and also aligns with your purpose.
- Your career provides a paycheck to support your lifestyle and the resources to support your purpose.
- Your career is dedicating your time to something that does not provide a paycheck.

My desire is to normalize and equalize all three of these. I do not believe one trumps another. One is not more admirable than another.

What matters is that you have done the important work of looking within to define what YOU want, not what you believe is expected of you. Once you define your favorite self and your favorite life, you can set out to create it.

Let's go back to the theater example. Maybe there is a fire in you craving to live your life in the arts full-time. Fan the flames. Maybe you recognize it as a hobby, and much like my passion for photography, it would be a gift to your art to not depend on it to provide for you. That is fine. Lastly, you may be the parent who is raising the next Viola Davis, and your role is to help provide her with the resources she needs to get where she needs to go. All three of these examples are beautiful lives.

Parent Guilt

I have found these concepts to be a regular struggle for mothers in particular. They are made to feel guilty and judged no matter what choice they make.

Women are often made to feel guilty for putting their children in daycare to pursue their careers. I regularly heard the phrase that daycare was "paying someone else to raise your kids." With my first child, I internalized this belief and tried to run a health and wellness business from home with my daughter. When she went to full-time childcare for the first time at age three, I felt like myself for the first time in years and instantly became a better mother. The boundaries allowed me clear windows of when I could focus on work and when I could enjoy my child, all the while knowing she was being loved and educated while I wasn't there. After that experience, my son, my second born, went into childcare with a stay-at-home mom at seven weeks, and I rarely felt guilty. I felt gratitude that he was loved in my absence. It was essential for my mental health and our family's livelihood.

In contrast, I regularly hear from mothers who stay home that they are made to feel guilty for a myriad of reasons, like not contributing financially to the household, not showing their daughters that women can have successful careers, or not living up to their potential. I want to call B.S. on all of it. There is no reason for any parent to feel guilty for doing what is best for their family. Part of unleashing your favorite self is owning your story. Define what is your favorite life, step into it, and own it. Set an example for others that this way of living, whichever is right for you, can be fulfilling and rewarding.

I didn't mean to leave dads out of this part of the conversation, but the reality is they get praised either way. When they show up to work with a five-week or even five-day-old baby at home, no one asks, "Who's watching the baby for you while you're at work?" And when Dad becomes a full-time stay-at-home parent, the comments I've heard are always, "Wow! That's so awesome you're supporting your partner's career!"

The issue I have heard from fathers is how these gender stereotypes have hurt them in the workplace. Many companies are improving, but some still make it a challenge to be an involved parent. Whereas the stereotypes in the workplace may be that moms need flexibility to accommodate children's needs, the reality is dads do, too. When a child is sick, and a parent needs to stay home, the dad should also feel supported by his organization to be the caretaker. Dad may also need the flexibility to slip out to watch a preschooler perform or attend an award ceremony for their middle schooler. They may also need help with carpooling or shuffling to extracurriculars. The more we can lessen gender stereotypes and support parents in their unique situations, the more we can all thrive. Personally, our family's goal is for my business to reach the point where I can retire my husband. He would love to be a stay-at-home dad and exclusively focus on our household's needs.

If there's one takeaway from this entire book, I hope it is this concept: **there is no one right way to live, only a right way for you.**

Strengths Finders

There is a tool I want to share that ties all three of the career scenarios together and can be applicable no matter how you write your definition.

If you have not taken the *Clifton Strengths Assessment* by Gallup[10] (formerly known as Strengths Finder,) I cannot recommend it highly enough. They define 34 different strengths that exist and then assess what your individual top five strengths are.

In the three scenarios I gave regarding how people may have intertwined their purpose, career, and paycheck, I have found through my clients and others that individuals who are closely aligned with their strengths in their daily work are often the most fulfilled.

After I took this assessment for the first time, I understood why I had experienced so much resistance trying to fit into teams that didn't like change. My brain is wired to constantly think of new ideas and implement them, so being anywhere that is asking me to conform to the "way things have always been done" is a recipe for misery for them and for me.

The assessment is mostly used in the workplace, but you can apply it anywhere you spend your time and energy. It's helpful in family dynamics, and I have had extreme success applying it to my philanthropic endeavors.

Within a few months of the assessment, I walked away from that health and wellness business I had been trying to force into success for four years and accepted a job at a non-profit, where I stayed for the next four years. I never saw myself going back into an employee role after becoming an entrepreneur, but the gift of having a job opportunity that allowed me to use all top five of my strengths almost every day was too serendipitous.

Although I may have taken a controversial stance (in the personal growth and coaching world) in saying that I don't teach the idea that you need to align your purpose and paycheck, I will say that it's vital to live a life in alignment with your strengths. That particular job required all of my top five strengths, and I think that's why I enjoyed it so much.

That experience also taught me that your purpose can be intertwined with everything you do. My purpose is to help others grow. Sure, it wasn't as in alignment as coaching full-time is, but I was intentional with many of the relationships I built during that time to help others discover ways to grow, expand, and have more belief in themselves.

When it comes to natural talent on a sporting field, we can often pick out the teenagers who are headed to a Division 1 school or a professional career. However, the talents identified by the CliftonStrengths are almost entirely traits that we just think of as "no big deal."

I will not list all 34 here, but a handful of examples are discipline, consistency, futuristic, learner, activator, focus, intellection, input, empathy, includer, and so many other qualities.

I always thought I was broken, and something must be wrong with me that I am neither disciplined nor consistent. Probably half of my clients are attracted to my work because they also struggle with this and are eager to learn the hacks and skills I've created to be successful despite these struggles. It wasn't until I found CliftonStrengths that I realized I was not broken; those two traits were in my bottom ten. Nothing was wrong with me, and most likely, it would remain a struggle for the rest of my life. However, these qualities that I thought were no big deal were apparently superpowers I didn't realize I possessed. My responsibility was to look for more ways to use my strengths to make organizations, communities, and the world better.

For example, of the 34 strengths, harmony ranked number 32 for me. It's in my bottom three. Since childhood, I have been more likely to be the one who would disrupt a group dynamic than calm it. My number one strength is the activator, meaning I am hungry to turn ideas into action, move quickly, get things done, and see the results. Sometimes, in real life, this can look like a bull in a china shop.

However, when I had a twenty-year-old family member struggling to pick a college major, I encouraged her to take this assessment. Her number one trait was harmony. And it's true. When she is in the room, she can make everyone get along effortlessly. With a little research of her other strengths, combined with her interests, we were able to identify that she would excel as a kindergarten teacher. She didn't realize that she was special in this way. She had never considered that helping everyone get along was very challenging for some people (ahem, ahem, like me) but a necessity in our world.

Most likely, the trait you think is no big deal because it's so effortless is probably your superpower. Most of the strengths identified in this assessment are characteristics people are so naturally talented at they just assume it comes easily to everyone. My second trait is strategic thinking, which I never understood was unique. I just assumed everyone else's brains were also mapping out scenarios, connecting dots, and looking for patterns. Both my husband and I laughed when we saw that my number 33 out of 34 was consistency, but it was in his top five. No wonder we make a great team.

When building an organization, you want to make sure your team is diversified with many of the strengths having a seat at the table and respecting the perspectives that each of them brings.

In my experience working with clients, the ones who are the most miserable in their jobs and frustrated with their lives are the people who are trying to work outside of their strengths.

The dominant messaging for so long has centered around aligning your purpose, passion, and career. I would love to see the conversation pivot to aligning your career with your strengths.

I regularly get emails from Gallup, the creators of this assessment. One day, these words showed up in my inbox, and they said it best: "Imagine a world where every person knew their strengths. Where each person knew what they were uniquely good at and could appreciate the uniqueness of those around them. Imagine your boss assigning you and your team specific projects because they know the strengths of each of their employees. Imagine your family communicating in the most healthy, effective way because everyone knows what each person needs. It's hard to imagine fully, but it all starts with you."

The Deeper Calling

When I was in a youth group, they used to do these spiritual gift tests every year or two. It was similar to a personality test but meant to help you discover where you can best serve in the church.

Every. Single. Time. I took those tests I scored off the charts for a pastor. In high school, I started my own Bible studies and looked for opportunities where I could "share a testimony," which is basically the only time a woman was allowed to have a microphone and talk to the congregation.

What I really wanted to be when I grew up was a pastor. It felt so right for me. But I couldn't because I was born with a vagina instead of a penis. So that made me unqualified.

It wasn't until well into adulthood and after college that I realized there were other denominations that did allow women into their seminaries. Had I known that at seventeen, I probably would have made completely different life choices.

But instead, do you know what I was told? I was told that the hospitality committee was a great place for women to serve. We all have our place in the hands and feet of God, and making sure people feel welcome and get fed is just as important of a job.

Listen, people, I don't even cook great meals for myself or my own children. When Mama is in charge, your choices are limited. Also, I can be very friendly if I remember to turn on the smile light switch in my brain. Most of the time, I am in task brain. I am often in another world in my head or focused on the project at hand and completely forget to acknowledge the humans in the same room as me. I do NOT belong on the church hospitality committee. That. Is. Not. My. "Spiritual Gift."

Recently, I put the puzzle pieces together and realized I had subconsciously found my own unique way to use those gifts despite the church telling me I was unqualified.

As a life coach, I help people discover their true potential and navigate the complexities of life. I am a professional public speaker. I write. I teach. I am birthing a community. I help others find their spiritual solace. My job isn't terribly different from a pastor, just without the church politics and boxes they are put in. Every pastor/priest I've ever had an opportunity to have an intimate conversation with has a belief different than the widely accepted ones of their faith that they have to hide because if they speak their truth, they will fall victim to "church cannibalism." I have a friend who is a pastor's wife and uses that term to talk about how the church eats its own whenever they fall out of line. I'm also not on a mission to convert anyone into any belief system other than unleashing their favorite self. I have no agenda of who that may, so that's a stark contrast, too.

I share this with you because, in so many of my conversations, I hear of people who had desires when they were younger that got squashed by someone, somewhere. What they really, truly wanted to do in the world was seemingly not possible, or a door was closed in their face.

My challenge is always to lean in. Sometimes, they are held back by the belief that it's too late. Maybe they always wanted to go to law school but are now in their fifties. Okay…well, you're going to be in your 70s one day either way. You can either forge a path later in life, go to school at the same time as your kids, and have a 20+ career doing something that gives you life or not. But either way, the next twenty years are still going to pass by.

At other times, they may genuinely be unable to pivot a career but can still find ways to plug into their interest. I met a business owner who always wanted to go into the military but was told she couldn't. She now volunteers with local veteran organizations. She is a financial planner and goes around to different veteran groups, helping them understand how to manage their finances better for free.

The child you were is still inside of you. Whether you had a dream at five, fifteen, or twenty-five that was never given life, you still can pursue it. If you're reading this book, then that means that the little child is still alive. They didn't die. They just grew bigger bodies. They had the weight of adulthood added to their shoulders. But they are still you. You are still them, and you can breathe life into yourself now that you may have needed many years ago.

No, I cannot see a world where I am standing in front of a pulpit every Sunday. I don't want or even believe all the same things now that eighteen-year-old Sophia did. But I can honor the dreams that were there and breathe life into them in ways that are helpful now. I can acknowledge that I have always had a desire to serve, guide, teach, and speak. It will just look different and probably better.

Is there a faint whisper of a voice inside of you that has never really gone away? Is there a dream that has been smothered by doubt, skepticism, or closed doors? Is there any part of you that flourished when you were younger and is begging you to breathe life into it again? Is there any part of you that has always been curious about something in the world but never had permission to explore?

Do you need to write yourself a permission slip to take the first step in a new direction?

On Quitting

I love quitting. Yes, the author of a personal growth book just said she loves quitting. For years, I suffered from the ideology of "you only fail if you quit." This created a fear of failure inside of me and a determination to create success, even if it was the wrong fit. Successful entrepreneurs will tell you that sometimes, one of the wisest business moves you can make is to discover a bad investment quickly in the process. You can cut your losses early before it drains all your resources.

Walking away from my photography business was such a gift. In retrospect, I drug it out for years after the expiration date. It belonged in my life as a hobby, not as a career.

During my first pregnancy and through the first three years of my daughter's life, I hustled to build a product-based health and wellness business. I told everyone I knew that I was committed to this business for the rest of my life. I regularly shared all my hopes and dreams of what life would be like after I achieved my goals. I was too stubborn to admit I was a square peg in a round hole. I forced and plowed my way into growth.

Two years in, I had stopped enjoying the work but was too stubborn to walk away because I was already in so deep. A life coach asked me, "What if there is another way? What if you could still achieve all these goals in your life but take a different vehicle to get there?" It was such an obvious question. It was sitting right there in front of me. However, it was a question I had never asked myself. I was so afraid of the word quit and of admitting I had failed that I also dragged that business out years after its expiration date.

After four years of pouring my heart and soul into this business, I was finally sitting on the cusp of success. The momentum was coming, but instead, I let it slowly fade away. I was burned out, had lost all joy in the work, and couldn't imagine doing this work for the rest of my life. I knew I wanted to be a life coach but still felt wholly unworthy, and that's when the opportunity to work a W-2, more traditional, office job with a regular paycheck revealed itself.

The word quit has too strong of a stigma. Sometimes, life absolutely requires perseverance. I understand the importance of instilling in one another that we don't quit just because something has become challenging or we have hit a roadblock. But other times, unleashing your favorite self means you need to release a part of you that isn't working. That may involve quitting a job, a business, a relationship, a friendship, a project, a vice, a habit, or anything else that's getting in the way of creating the life you crave.

Next Steps

Do you have a clearer picture yet of your favorite self? What are they doing in the world? What lights them on fire? What brings them joy?

Today, are the choices you're making bringing you closer or taking you further away from that favorite self?

Look back to Chapter 2, and how you ranked your career spoke on a scale of 1-10. Taking this information into consideration, do you feel the number is still accurate, or would you adjust it? Do you want to write a new definition? Hop over to the journal to explore this more in-depth.

Chapter Nine:

FAMILY

When I do *Favorite Life Wheel* assessments with individuals, I find it uncommon to see a medium-ranked family spoke. These are the three most common responses I receive on this spoke:

- People rank their family between seven and nine. It's very strong, but they acknowledge there could be some room for improvement.

- They ask me if it just includes the people in their house or their extended family, too. Their home is good, but the conflicts with family members outside their home are a completely different conversation.

- They pause, go silent, and struggle to answer the question. They may get choked up. They may get sad. They may go into shame.

Either way, it's always hard for them to admit to me a number when it's in the one to three range for family.

This tells us so much about the role that family plays in our lives. In most of the other spokes, if it's a one to three, people just own it and keep going. Self-care is low. They usually just laugh, inferring it's a ridiculous idea they could ever prioritize themselves before others. Body spoke low? They tell me they know they should be eating better and exercising but just aren't. Their career is low? They're likely aware the life they're living isn't sustainable, and usually, it's a significant reason they contacted a life coach.

But family? I've yet to have someone chuckle when they tell me that one is low. They're rarely quick to move to the next spoke. I've struck a pain cord, and we need to pause for a moment. Why? Why is our interaction with this spoke so different?

This pain runs deep because we are humans. We are designed this way. We want to love and be loved. It's part of the human experience to crave a group of people to call your family, know that they love you, and feel safe and supported by them. If these basic human needs are not being met, pain is inevitable.

If you feel pain in this spoke, I hope this chapter breathes some hope into your life. I hope you will gain more confidence that there is a path for you to create a ten here.

If you fall into group one, the seven to ten range, most likely, you already know what you need to do. A little more intention can often get it to your ten. Improving this spoke often involves reviewing your habits. Creating a

FAMILY

couple of daily or weekly intentional actions could greatly increase this spoke. Do you need to call someone more often to check in? Do you need to put some standing plans on the calendar? Is your family just too busy and you need to say no to some things to increase the time spent at home together? Do you need to create some rituals that involve something everyone likes to do together? If you look at your habits and your calendar, you usually know what would improve this area. It becomes a matter of making it a higher priority.

I have shared a couple of times in this book that when I first did my wheel, I didn't realize which spokes were actually the ones creating my feeling of being "stuck." The Family spoke was one of them. I kept hoping that if I just ignored the relationship conflicts in my life, they would magically fix themselves.

Problems in our lives that we ignore rarely fix themselves. More often, ignoring them just makes them grow larger.

For this reason, I don't want to write a chapter filled with all the fun habits that have added value to our lives. There are already so many books, Pinterest posts, and Instagram accounts dedicated to these ideas. I am confident that if you are searching for ideas or inspiration for how to improve quality time with your family members, a quick Google search will fill your mind with inspiration.

Instead, I concluded that discussing the most common pain points would add much more value to you.

Defining Your Family

Your definition of family is anyone you want to define as family. Some family members come to you through blood, and others are chosen from the heart. There are reasons that sometimes people must release their blood relative(s) and create a new chosen family. I highly recommend investing in therapy before going "no contact" with a family member. The pain is often as grief-ridden as experiencing the death of a loved one, but it is sometimes someone's only option to get the healing they need and deserve.

Recently, when we were having a family dinner, my daughter was complaining about something her little brother was doing. My husband smiled and said, "Do you realize that your mom is the only family member I chose? Everyone else, including you, I'm just stuck with. I didn't get to pick most of my family, just like you didn't get to pick your brother. You just learn how to get along."

She made a confused face, so he clarified, "I fell in love with your mom and chose to marry her. But I didn't get to pick my parents. I didn't get to pick my brother and sisters. When I married your mom, I also gained all of her family as my family. Mommy didn't get to pick her family members either. And guess what else? We didn't even get a say in who any of our siblings married. Or the kids they have. We just had family members added to our lives that we didn't choose. We love them, and we learn how to get along. Just like how you will spend the rest of your life learning how to get along with your brother."

He was right. I had never considered the fact that he was indeed the only person I chose. If we do not include our grandparents, aunts, uncles, or cousins, our two families combined are twenty-five people, and we each choose only one of those people.

All of that is to say, why would we ever in a million years walk through our lives expecting that it should be easy breezy to get along like best friends?

In most of the other relationships in our lives, we have some control and influence. We often pick friendships based on things we have in common or the types of people to whom we feel drawn. With coworkers, if the workplace culture is toxic, we can find a new job. We join community organizations based on shared interests or causes.

However, when it comes to family, we may get lucky and share common interests. We may get lucky and have personalities that mesh well. But often, we are figuring out how to share life with people despite disagreeing on sports teams, religion, politics, values, conspiracy theories, or what defines a good versus terrible TV series.

Whereas we may not be able to choose who we are related to, we can choose who we include in the definition of our family spoke. These are the core relationships we want to invest in.

Let's circle back to why the *Favorite Life Wheel* exists. The *Favorite Life Wheel* is a measuring system to help us assess each area of our lives, how they are interconnecting, and determine how to grow all the spokes to a strong number. A wheel with ten strong spokes is a thriving life.

That said, I recommend physically writing onto a piece of paper the names of each of the people who you will have in mind when you rank this spoke. That aunt you see once a year during the holidays who gets under your skin with her insensitive comments? You don't have to force yourself into a relationship with her to have a thriving life.

Whereas *Insensitive Aunt* may be easy to leave out of your family definition, there may be some name in your life that you struggle with. Some clarifying questions to ask yourself are:

Is this relationship salvageable?

Is the other person also invested in growth and working on the relationship, or am I the only one putting in effort?

Would it be healthier for me to release them from the expectations I have for my core family spoke members and allow them to be someone still in my life but with a little more distance?

You May Need a New 10

By this point in the book, you have probably caught on to a central theme. Much of our suffering in life comes from the "shoulds" we have internalized. We receive messaging and input from so many sources, giving us a perception of how things "should" look in life. When it comes to family dynamics, so many people think they are failing because it doesn't look perfect. What if we changed the expectation? What if it's not supposed to be perfect? What if we accept that it's a complicated mess, and each person is probably doing their best?

When you turn off the screens and have in-depth conversations with other people, almost everyone has some messy area of their family lives. As I wrack my brain right now trying to think of one example of a client or friend who has no complicated situation in their family, no one is coming to mind.

FAMILY

What if our definition of a ten wasn't handed to us, but we created it on our own?

What if we acknowledge that our parents were humans and made mistakes? What if we acknowledge that we are humans and give ourselves grace when we make mistakes?

What if some of the suffering in the family spoke is because we are comparing ourselves to other people, media, and internalized messaging of how the family should be versus just accepting and loving what we have?

Social media will send you down a quick shame cycle if you start comparing what other families are doing, affording, experiencing, and achieving when your situation looks completely different.

The modern family often involves divorce, bonus parents, two moms or two dads, a single parent, a grandparent or aunt/uncle in the parent role, or many other scenarios. There may be mental health challenges or an illness in one person that affects every single person in the family.

I see many people causing themselves suffering because of a thought about how someone in their lives "should" be behaving. It could be abandonment and wanting someone to return who has left. It could be an addiction and wanting someone to give up their vice. It could be neglect or many other circumstances. All of these examples are often traumatic. Most often, the thoughts around how others should behave are lighter. We may wish they would make different decisions with their lives, like how they spend their time or money, the values they choose, or anything else we disagree with.

Many people are labeling themselves with a gap in their family spoke because of someone else's life choices. If any part of your gap between where you are and where you want to be hinges on some other person in your life behaving differently, you probably need to look within at what is in your control, what is not, and evaluate your definition.

What if the definition was changed to acknowledge that they're not able to be present, and a definition was written that involved loving and being loved by the people who are showing up? If that list is only one or two people, that's enough.

What is your definition of a ten in your family spoke? I recommend writing your definition of your favorite life you would love to share with those people on your list. For an even greater impact, talk to those family members about it. Share your definition of ten with them. Do they share the same vision? Is there a better vision that you can work toward together? Setting expectations that involve others, but they have no idea what they are, will often lead to unnecessary disappointment.

It's Not Others, It's You

If you find yourself regularly bothered by the choices others make, I cannot recommend the book *Codependent No More* by Melody Beattie[11] highly enough. I would have never described myself as someone who was codependent. I only picked up the book because three authors I love, each in different episodes of their podcasts, talked about how reading that book was so life-changing, humbling, and a giant punch to the gut. After seeing a trend, I thought, "If I find myself resonating with these women so powerfully, and they each learned from this book, maybe there is stuff in there I need to hear."

And OOF. Yep. The book showed me how I had actually been healing from codependent behaviors for over a decade, and I didn't even know that was the language to describe what was happening. In her book, Beattie defines codependency as "one who has let another person's behavior affect him or her, and who is obsessed with controlling that person's behavior."

She also goes on to explain that a powerful antidote is self-love. The more we turn our energy to discovering our needs and meeting those needs, the easier it is to release ourselves from other's actions.

In full transparency, I did quite the happy dance when I got to that part. I knew that learning how to love and care for myself had healed so much of me. As I explained to my husband, the book showed me that a younger version of myself had more than 50% of the symptomatic behaviors of codependency, but the work I have done led me to self-assess at below 20% of them left to clean up.

If there is one thing I've learned the most from my many years of cleaning up the parts of my family spoke that caused me stress, it's this…

It was always me.

I don't mean that we have to take responsibility for what others do to us, but we are always responsible for our own healing. Our own thoughts. Our own words. Our own actions. The suffering I was experiencing was always within my control to end.

Side note: I am referring to my emotions in adulthood that caused me suffering. This reference does not apply to children who genuinely cannot remove themselves from difficult circumstances. The statement "it was always me" refers to taking ownership of our healing in adulthood.

Each time I have hired a therapist or read a book to help me work on something that is causing me stress, I end up realizing that I am the one who has to change. Because we cannot change anyone but ourselves.

When I have shared this sentiment with clients before, they are sometimes quick to jump into a defensive posture, "But you don't know my dad! He's so controlling and so rude! It's him who needs to change, not me!"

Okay. Maybe Dad is controlling and rude, but are you standing there accepting it? You can only control yourself. If you are old enough to have moved out of your dad's house, then you can set boundaries of what you will and will not accept and leave the house when it's too inappropriate or end the phone call. You can do the inner healing work of separating from your dad's controlling grip and not letting him micromanage your life. We'll talk more about boundaries in a bit.

Passing the Baton

There was a moment in my childhood that was important enough that my brain stored it in its long-term memory. However, it took me twenty years to comprehend just how profound of a moment it was.

When I was around twelve, my younger sister was eight, and my brother was seven. We were all in the backseat. We started bickering about who knows what. My mom probably warned us. She probably asked us to stop, but the part I remember is she lost her patience. She flung her right arm into the backseat and just started hitting whatever she could find. Mom

NEVER EVER did that. It was a "just wait 'til your father gets home" kind of household. So, we knew we had pushed too far.

I remember riding in silence for a little while, and my mom was crying. Then (maybe she pulled over, maybe not, it was a time-stood-still moment) she broke the silence and, through the tears said, "This is what I need you three to understand. Sometimes I make mistakes, and I get it wrong, but the way I mother you is 100% better than how your maw-maw raised me. But let me tell you this— her life was HARD. Things you will never know or understand. And I'm certain that she did the best she could. She was a 100% better mother to me than her mom was to her. My expectation is that each of you will follow the example that was set for you, and you will take my good, leave my bad, and be a 100% better parent, too."

I've shared that memory a few times with people, and it always pierces the heart. I think it's because in that moment she summarized the journey of humanity. To just keep making things better. And she summarized what it means to be a parent. To constantly feel like you're getting it right and wrong on a daily basis.

When we look at our family histories, many of us share this exact same lineage. For so many families, each generation is doing the best they can with the knowledge, resources, and capacities they have. All we can expect of ourselves is to do our best.

What if we approached our perceptions through this lens? What if we gave more grace to the people around us and accepted that what we are seeing may be their best? What if we stopped expecting them to be perfect? What if we dropped the unachievable standards displayed in our culture and just decided our role was to carry the baton? To receive what was handed to us and carry it closer to the finish line?

I know I've made a lot of mistakes. I've said words that hurt people. I've been hurt by the words of others. I've reacted out of emotion before thinking something through. I've been hurt by the actions of others who didn't think something through themselves. I've been too busy and distracted to be intentional. I've been forgotten by people who were exhausted, busy, and distracted.

Now, I regularly remind myself that I don't have to get it right all the time. I just need to keep the baton moving forward. I am grateful for all my ancestors who, over the generations, have carried their baton to get us to where we are now. And I will honor them by making the improvements that are asked of me and my generation.

Boundaries

In the last few years, the conversation around boundaries has exploded. Part of this explosion is a result of more people gaining access to therapy[12], the decreasing stigma around going to therapy[13], and social media making it easier for therapists to disseminate education. I was thirty-one years old before I read my first book on boundaries, and it was very eye-opening to me. I could see clearly where I had a lack of boundaries, but also where I was overstepping other's lives who didn't know how to set boundaries with me.

On a regular basis, I recommend the book *Set Boundaries, Find Peace: A Guide to Reclaiming Yourself*[14] by Nedra Glover Tawwab. It's not the be-all and end-all of books that can help family dynamics, but learning how to set boundaries well and clarify your needs is often the first step. Regularly, when my clients share conflicts with me that are creating challenging dynamics for them, this book brings them clarity on what they can do next.

Through my conversations with people discovering why they aren't living their favorite lives, I have found it to be common that people are not aware of what their needs are. If we have not done the work to know how to best care for ourselves, how can we expect those around us to know? Oftentimes, people who love us try to be helpful, but their actions (or inactions) are not what we crave.

This is yet another reason I love the *Favorite Life Wheel* concept of showing us how all areas of our lives are integrated. The more you improve your self-care spoke and understand what you need to pour from an overflowing cup, the more you can share that information with those around you. The book *The Five Love Languages* by Gary Chapman is frequently recommended to address the idea of meeting each other's needs. However, it's my opinion that it barely scratches the surface. There are many more than five needs, and it's our responsibility to explore what ours are.

Do you need more communication but hate the phone? What can that look like in your relationships? Do you feel overwhelmed by people and need to prioritize more time to be alone? Having that awareness allows you to know how much time you can be together before you need to go home and restore your energy. This may be hard for someone to understand who gains energy by being with others and assumes if you loved them, you would crave more time together.

Is it possible that you and someone in your family have completely different definitions of what a ten in this spoke would look like, so you are always creating friction? Have you done the work to define your top values in life, and do you know what theirs are? What if, in an attempt to live according to the values you place as the highest priority, you are constantly offending theirs? Someone who values privacy may not appreciate someone who values open communication and vulnerability. Is it possible for those two people to respect the other one's needs and find ways to communicate that don't feel invasive to the other person? What does common ground look like?

The bottom line is: We are not mind readers.

Expectations that are **not** expressed cannot be met. If you expect the other person to always call you, but they aren't aware that's what you want from them, you will have created your own suffering by sitting alone at home waiting for the phone to ring.

I get it, expressing what we want can feel very vulnerable. It takes courage to put yourself out there and risk how someone may respond. In her book *Rising Strong*[15], Brene Brown says, "Integrity is choosing courage over comfort; choosing what is right over what is fun, fast, or easy; and choosing to practice our values rather than simply professing them."

Despite the fact that I have a very assertive personality and can speak my opinions and needs easier than most of the people I know, I STILL am regularly biting my lip, tolerating the pit in my stomach, or going silent and venting my frustrations to someone other than the person I am frustrated with. We all do this.

Because this is a growth area I am actively working on, and I have a dear friend who is also working on this in her life, I recently bought us both key chains that say, "Courage Over Comfort." It's a daily reminder to listen to that pit in the stomach or say no to betraying myself with silence. As Cheryl Richardson said, "If you avoid conflict to keep the peace, you go to war within yourself."

I reference that quote almost daily to remind me to tap into my courage. Most often, the courage I need is to use my voice to speak up for myself. I rarely run away from conflict when I feel the need to defend someone else. But defending myself? That is my growth. And I know it's hard for so many others.

We often tell ourselves the story that it's not worth the tension. We can just walk away and deal with it on our own. The silent suffering takes a tremendous toll on not only our bodies but our relationships as well. We are sending a message that we are okay accepting behaviors that we actually are not.

Professional Help

If you have a low number in this spoke, I cannot recommend professional help highly enough. There are therapists who specialize in family relationships, but also ones who specialize in helping you heal from things in the past.

So many of the topics that I have touched on are brushing the surface of what therapists have deeply studied on how to help people move through their obstacles.

As mentioned in Chapter 3, The Mind, I have done talk therapy and EMDR. My most recent therapist did both, and I found that to be the right fit for me. The EMDR work allows us to go into the memories of the past and rewrite them in a way that helps us heal.

I didn't realize I was someone who was deeply affected by trauma because nothing violent or "major" had ever happened to me. Through this work, I discovered that I was holding onto several traumas. I was able to see how my brain had rewired its belief systems about how the world works after those encounters. The symptoms of those experiences were still showing up decades later.

I had immense amounts of unprocessed grief from losing my brother at five, my grandfather at six, and my grandmother, who I idolized, at age fourteen. In hindsight, it should have been a red flag that I never cried after my grandmother died. We were extremely close. I just thought I had thick skin or death had been so normalized for me, but now I understand it was a trauma response. I also worked through hurtful words, some bullying I endured in middle school, and old conflicts with family members.

I share all of this with you, the reader, with only one motivation in mind. My desire is to normalize the idea that each one of our brains is wired in a specific way because of the experiences we have had. Some of those experiences may have been painful. Depending on the circumstances and how they were handled, those experiences may still be shaping how you interact with others. If so, there are experts who can help you change.

FAMILY

Meet Sandra

Sandra reached out to me for coaching because her self-care spoke was at a one. She had spent her entire life living to serve other people. She gave her work and her children everything she had, but she didn't take care of herself. She longed for more pleasure and joy but didn't even know where to start.

When we first started coaching, Sandra ranked her family spoke high. But as we dove into what was going on in all the moving parts of her life, she realized that a significant piece of her ability to grow her self-care involved her family.

For most of her children's lives, she had been a single mom. Her adult children adored her, and she adored them. But one day, she shared with me that it was becoming harder and harder to fight off the emotion of jealousy. Both of her children had met their future spouses and no longer needed her to be the person they shared the details of their everyday lives with. She found herself waiting for the phone to ring or waiting for a text to come through that wasn't coming.

I absolutely love the emotion of jealousy. It's one of the best teachers we are given. Whenever jealousy arrives, she reveals to us something we need to know about ourselves. She holds up a mirror for us to see our deepest desires that are not being met. Her wisdom has guided me many times to listen better to my true self.

In Sandra's case, the power was in seeing that her life was shifting seasons. She wasn't going to be the first phone call anymore. We ran a Thought Wheel (see Chapter 4) to see what her feelings were underneath. She was able to see that her brain planted the A.N.T. (remember from Chapter 2, that's an Automatic Negative Thought) that her kids didn't love her as much anymore. We were able to debunk that really quickly and identify it as the lie it was. She looked at what was within her control and what actions she could take. By the time we spoke two weeks later, she had made a 180-degree turnaround.

She decided to talk to her kids about how she was struggling. Her kids reassured her how much they loved her, and they talked about new ways their communication could look. Yes, this was a new season. No, the old patterns and behaviors weren't going to work anymore. But with everyone being open, they were able to discuss how they could meet each other's needs in ways that served them all.

Sandra also realized with this seasonal shift, it was true that her kids didn't need her as much. They still needed her, of course, but she could acknowledge that this season increased how much freedom she had for herself. She started looking inward for how she could use her time and what would bring her pleasure and joy.

She began to understand that her definition of who was in her family and her definition of a ten wasn't serving her. Most of her family of origin (the family you are born into) had been taking, but not giving her entire lifetime. She was exhausted from always caring about relatives who never reciprocated any love, effort, or support. After decades of the same patterns, she realized that she could still love them deeply but release them from this spoke. She wasn't responsible for cleaning up their messes, coming to their rescue, or solving their problems when they had never once cared about any of her messes, obstacles, or problems. By naming what was her true reality and rewriting her family as her husband and kids, she lifted a heavy weight off her shoulders. She had felt responsible for carrying that load for fifty years.

Within a few months of working together and making some tweaks in the family spoke and others, she grew her self-care rating from a one to a seven. She took four trips in three months and even took an entire week's vacation from work to sit at home and rest. She could not remember the last time she had taken a vacation from work, while never checking her phone or email.

Sandra applied the principles we talked about in this chapter: clearer communication, boundaries, revised expectations, and new definitions. She had the goal of increased self-care and more joy in her life, but making these changes overflowed into every single spoke on her wheel. Not only is she enjoying her career more, but her body has started changing and she's losing the weight she's tried to lose for decades because she's valuing herself more. It's all connected.

What's Next

Revisit your *Favorite Life Wheel* assessment from the beginning of the book. With these new thoughts in mind, do you need to change your definition or list of names you're thinking about when you evaluate the family spoke?

What is the next step to get you closer to your 10? Is it being intentional with some new habits? Reading a book that dives into the details of your personal struggles? Having a hard conversation with someone? Clarifying your personal values and asking them what they value the most?

Quite frequently, when it comes to the family spoke, we adopt beliefs that this spoke isn't at a ten because of something to do with someone else. How can you take your power back? How can you claim complete ownership over your life?

Chapter Ten:

FRIENDSHIP

Following a nearly 80-year study[16] by Harvard University examining how to live a long, healthy, and happy life, Dr. Robert Waldinger, the fourth director of the study, did a Ted Talk in 2015 sharing the results. I highly recommend watching the full presentation, but here are a couple of quotes that I want to draw attention to, "Taking care of your body is important, but tending to your relationships is a form of self-care too. That, I think, is the revelation."

He explains that as of 2015, 19 of the over 700 men in the study were still alive and in their mid-nineties. It was not their good genes, income, healthy eating, or workout routines that predicted whether they would outlive their peers. The common denominator between the men who lived long, happy lives was the quality of their relationships.

"The people who were the most satisfied in their relationships at age fifty were the healthiest at age eighty," he shared.

If you dive into the research yourself or watch the Ted Talk, you will see that marriage and family relationships are frequently mentioned. But here's the reason I am bringing up this study in the friendship chapter: "Loneliness kills," he said. "It's as powerful as smoking or alcoholism."

There are other studies[17] as well that support the notion that loneliness is detrimental to our health.

With this awareness, how can I consider myself a great life coach and not make sure that people are prioritizing their friendships? Of course, family is important, as we discussed in the last chapter, but our friends add so much joy and fill many of the gaps in our lives.

However, adult friendships are complicated. In our youth, making friends is more natural. Most people grow up going to schools where they are surrounded by the same people every weekday and naturally form friendships as a result of the long periods of time spent together. As we enter adulthood, some of those friendships from our youth may last, but many do not.

I am regularly asked to speak at events, usually conferences, and thus far, the vast majority of my keynotes and workshops have been given to rooms of all women. At almost every event, I will walk the audience through the *Favorite Life Wheel* assessment. After they rank their spokes from 1-10, I will often ask the room to raise their hands if their friendship spoke is a 5 or below. I do not ask this question to embarrass anyone. My motivation is to show them they are not alone. To date, every room has been around one-third to one-half of the audience.

This antidotal observation may not be research, but it does breathe hope into those who are struggling in their friendships to know it's hard for many others as well.

My clients who are working on growth in this area will often share thoughts full of misconceptions and assumptions with me. They often assume that everyone else has friend groups that are hanging out a lot or people who are picking up the phone and calling each other but not them, or naturally are better at friendships than they are. Sure, a percentage of the population has cultivated that lifestyle, but all, or even most? Not so much. What do we know about the word assume? In case you have missed this memo, ass-u-me. It makes an ass out of you and me.

I get it. For me, this has been a spoke that has fluctuated all over like a rollercoaster, often impacted by transitions in my seasons of life.

In recent years, my pain in the friendship spoke finally got significant enough that I was ready to do something about it. The frustration over wishing things looked different than their reality reached a point where I was ready to put in the work to find solutions. As I mentioned at the beginning of this book, I cannot hand you a perfect step-by-step guide to your life, but I will share with you my recipes from my cookbook. If you like them, you can try them out. If you don't, I'm confident that you will find a recipe elsewhere that works for you. If you gain nothing else from this chapter, I hope it is this nugget:

This spoke matters as much as all the others. It's not a spoke that should be put on the back burner. Your season of life may dictate what you can realistically set as your definition of a 10, but you do not need to settle for a low number. If your other spokes are drowning you, this is often the spoke that gets neglected. However, it's also the spoke that can pull you out of the river when you can no longer keep your head above water. Please don't suffer alone. Most likely, there is someone also fighting for their lives nearby and you two have a much better chance of survival if you link arms than if you keep trying to do it all by yourself.

When Friendship Hurts

From the outside looking in, I appear to be someone who probably kicks ass at the friendship spoke. I appear to be extremely outgoing, and always socializing. Back when AIM* was the predominant way we communicated, my username was SocialButterly777. Maybe it's the personality I was born with, maybe it's the result of starting at new schools five times between K-12 where I knew no one and was forced to figure out how to meet new people, but meeting new people and making new friends is both easy and fun for me.

I'm a person who has made friends in a grocery store. I'm a person who never meets a stranger. I'm a person who goes to a networking event and can talk to someone I have never met and quickly form a connection and have stimulating conversations. I hate small talk, so I tend to start with simple questions and then suddenly find myself absorbing someone's life story and listening to their hopes, dreams, or fears. I do this without

---

*AIM stands for AOL Instant Messenger. It was much like text messaging, or an Instagram Direct Message (DM) but on the computer. In the late 1900's and early 2000's, this was the predominate way young people kept in touch with their friends outside of school. The elder millennial generation and younger Gen X most heavily used this form of communication.

intention and have created many awkward situations by accident. I just genuinely enjoy people and find everyone's unique stories and experiences fascinating.

Because of these qualities, I spent many years thinking I had tons of friends. If I wanted to do something fun, I had a wide circle of friends to extend an invitation to. I could find company whenever I desired.

And then, life hit. I've already shared with you the story of my daughter being born at the same time we hit rock bottom. During one of the hardest seasons of our lives, some of my friends showed up big time. Others vanished from my life. It took me years to unravel that pain, to understand why, how, and what to do next.

It happened again when my son was born. I had a horribly challenging pregnancy while my husband traveled over 50% of the time for work. I struggled to take care of our four-year-old. Then, our son contracted RSV at two months old. He was in the hospital for eleven days, intubated for five of them, and we almost lost him. In that year, friends had many opportunities to show up. Some people I was pouring a lot of myself into at the time managed to skip the baby shower, never come visit after he was born, and during the hospital stay, they commented on a Facebook post that they were praying for us. Meanwhile, the friends and family who carried us through that difficult year were the ones I most often took for granted.

My relationships were wide, but they were not deep. Despite loving deep conversations, I was spreading myself thin rather than heavily investing in a core group.

Here's the irony of the situation. As much as I love deep conversations and live my life as an open book, I am actually quite closeted and protective of certain parts of myself, including my deepest fears and pains, the full vision of my big dreams, the driving forces behind why I do many of the things I do, my spiritual journey, and other intimate details. There are things that friends and family will learn about me for the first time within these pages.

Occasionally, I would find people who made me feel safe. I would open up and share these intimacies with them. In retrospect, I didn't realize I was doing it, but I was defining them as my inner circle because I opened up to them. The biggest mistake I ever made was *I never asked them how they defined their inner circle. I just assumed I was in theirs if they were in mine.*

I would love on and prioritize these people in a way that I didn't give freely to others. However, because of my social butterfly personality, I think they just assumed I gave in this way to everyone in my life. They just assumed they were one of my hundreds of friendships because I never directly told them how special they were to me.

And then, something would happen. They would hold an event for their friends, and I didn't make the list. I would have a major event happen in my life, and they would assume my hundreds of other friends were making sure I was taken care of. Somehow, some way, something would occur that made it glaringly obvious that I misunderstood. They were in my inner circle, but I was not in theirs.

FRIENDSHIP

Glennon Doyle talks about friendship a lot on her podcast "We Can Do Hard Things." She put language to what I had spent my entire life wrestling with. To paraphrase, her friendship rants sound something like:

> Friendship is so hard because we don't know the rules. What are the rules? What are the expectations? When we enter a romantic relationship, at some point, we have "the talk." Are we putting a label on this? Are we exclusive, or is this open?
>
> There are books and experts galore teaching us how to meet our partner's needs and communicate better. And then, if you decide to enter into a marriage, you sign an actual contract. You legally bind yourselves together.
>
> If the relationship isn't working out anymore, you can get more legal paperwork establishing that the relationship is over. Especially if children are involved, you have explicit conversations about what this relationship will look like post the end. When going through a breakup, people know you are hurting and will console you and sympathize with your pain.
>
> But friendship? How do we know we have moved from acquaintances who see each other a lot to the label of friends? How do we know if we are basic friends or inner circle friends? How do I know what you expect from me? How do you know what I expect from you?

These conversations are not normalized.

My husband does not share my pain. He is not a social butterfly. He has a small handful of friends that he keeps on a shortlist and pours heavily into them. There's no gray area. There are no assumed expectations. But also, they're men. They are not discussing the inner depth of their emotions. They're talking about their fantasy football teams. They're not sending each other gifts for major life events; they're texting each other funny GIFs.

This female friendship thing is brutal, and it's hard for him to resonate. "She hasn't come to meet your daughter, who is now a year old? Why does that matter? She probably doesn't like babies," or, "She invited someone else to the concert to see your favorite band and didn't tell you about the show. Okay. Why are you upset? You didn't even love the band enough to look up their schedule. Why was it her responsibility to tell you they were coming to a city three hours away?" And then after that triple date, "So they didn't invite us to grab dessert with them after but posted it on social the next day, don't take it so personally." How can you not take that personally!

The only time that he ever understood the pain and just looked at me with the most pitiful, helpless eyes was, "Your best friend came into town for the first time in a decade and drove past your exit on the interstate and didn't even stop to say hi." I remember that day at work vividly. I saw the social media post while at work. I just went into the single-stall bathroom, locked the door, sat on the floor with my back against the wall and bawled.

Even just recalling these experiences, I have tears streaming down my cheeks. I know, guys, I know. Friendships can be so, so hard. And so confusing.

I'm not naïve enough to think I'm innocent here. Because of how confusing these dynamics get, I am sure that someone, somewhere out there, probably has a story about how I neglected them when they most desired my attention, and I caused them deep pain. Actually, I don't even have to assume. I already know.

The friend who drove past my exit…I didn't know how to show up for her when she was going through depression. I didn't realize I was the only person she confided in, and at that time, depression wasn't widely talked about. I thought she was describing a mood she was in, not a mental health crisis. She later recalled the pain and told me, "You just asked me if I had tried meditation and changed the topic." Ouch.

Or that friend who found someone else to go on a road trip to the concert with. I later found out why. The last time Hanson (Yes, they still perform. Yes, I've seen them multiple times as an adult) was in town, I was too busy trying to be ten places at once that I asked my extremely introverted friend to carpool with another friend of mine, she had never met. The day before the concert, I told her to meet me at the show that was an hour away because I needed to come late. In my head, these two people had about 100 things in common, and I was basically setting up the best blind date friendship opportunity ever. From her perspective, she felt completely rejected by me and insulted that I would spring her deepest fear on her, which was talking to strangers.

Have you all noticed the pattern yet? Last year when I decided I would finally figure out how to be a better friend and get my friendship needs met one way or another, I had to analyze where it had failed before.

Can you see the common denominator in every single one of these stories?

We are all craving to be seen by the people we love.

Notice me when I am in pain. Notice me when my life is transitioning, and I feel so alone. Notice my fears. Help me feel safe. Notice me when I crave to be celebrated.

Notice me.

And yet, let's add another level of complexity to the matter.

Notice me in a way that will make me feel like I have been seen.

Well, shit.

We are all running around in our busy lives, juggling all ten spokes on our wheels, struggling to feel our own feelings and prioritize our own self-care, but we are also supposed to read everyone else's minds and know what they need better than they know themselves?

Cool. Cool. Got it. Yes, let me jump right on that.

There have been times that I so desperately wanted to just shout. "I give up! Here. I am waving the white flag. I surrender." I will just give up on expecting it's possible to have intimate friendships and will figure out how to live a happy life with just my family and work and surface-level relationships. I will own the title of bad friend and let all of you do that shit together. I'll just take care of myself.

But I know better. I know that's not how it works. I know that I crave to share love with others and feel loved in return.

Meeting our Needs

I know that I have really quirky interests. Neither my husband nor any members of my family find the same things fascinating as I do. They will not get excited talking to me for hours about whatever my latest area of growth is. I just purchased my first concert ticket in ten years (shout out to Jake Wesley Rogers). However, I've purchased tickets to several events to listen to authors or thought leaders speak. Attending a conference about something I'm interested in? That's riveting. But a band? That's stressful and overstimulating to me in my thirties. Invite me to your book club, not your happy hour.

This is where our friends come in. We have an opportunity to build a life with people who also love the same quirky things we do. We can have our needs met by a wide, diverse group of people. It's not my partner's duty to suffer through an event with me when he is deeply introverted. Earlier this year, my friend Deanna and I went as each other's date to a ball. We got dolled up, put on false lashes and evening gowns, and hit the dance floor. My husband put the kids down and played video games with his friends. We were both in our joy.

Just like the family spoke, I had to come to the humble realization that it was exclusively up to me to fix my friendship woes. I was the only common denominator between all the times I had been hurt and hurt others.

Much like the self-care spoke and so many other times this philosophy has come up in this book, I had to begin with identifying my needs. I had to look at myself in the mirror and answer some really vulnerable questions:

- What are the things that make me feel the most seen?
- What do my friends do that makes me feel the most loved?
- What hurts the most?
- What are things that might be okay to other people but are boundaries I cannot have crossed in my world?
- What kind of friend am I willing to be?
- What value can I consistently offer?
- What are the needs they may have that I will probably not be able to meet?
- What brings me the absolute most joy to contribute to a friendship?
- How do I identify the difference between the inner circle friends, the good friends, and the acquaintance friends?

Knowing the answers to these questions helped clarify for me where to invest my time and energy. However, I want to warn you that discovering my own answers was about a three-year experiment. I didn't know all of them when I started. I had to let the answers come to light.

I cannot tell you the "right" answers. They do not exist. Think of this process as rewriting a new definition of a ten for the friendship spoke. Your ten will be clarifying what it looks like for you to have your needs met and what will bring you the most joy in how you love your friends.

FRIENDSHIP

My examples

I will share with you some of the things I learned about myself in this exploration process.

When I first started to experiment with finding my friendship needs, I started mirroring. It was the easiest action. I would reflect back to others what they were showing me. I would love them the way they loved me. This weeded out the relationships that were fully dependent on me to keep them alive. In earlier seasons of my life, and I'm sure again when my kids are grown, I will have the mental capacity to carry the initiation weight. In this season, I only have the bandwidth to support shared responsibility friendships.

The birth of both children and then a couple of other season shifts taught me that for my inner circle, I need people who show up in times of need and celebration or communicate to me why they can't. But the silence is too loud for my soul.

I learned that an inner circle friend for me has to be someone who texts back. Maybe not right away, maybe even three days later, but eventually. The lack of responsiveness brings out the worst of me. The responsiveness gives me a sense of security. I know that there are people who don't text. It's fine. It really is. We can still be friends. I am still going to love you. It's just that my anxiety cannot handle having you in my top few relationships I invest in for my own self-preservation.

I have one friend who told me, "If ever I don't text back, it's because I got distracted and legit forgot. If too much time passes, just text me again. I promise to never be offended." I'll send her a "poke" several hours later or the next day and know that no one's feelings are hurt. Sometimes, she will even see a text from me and respond, "Pinning this." Which is code for requires too much thought. I don't have that kind of energy right now. Or maybe she's in the middle of chaos with her three kids. It's a way of saying, "Let's circle back when I have capacity." Honesty is such a gift.

I also learned, after going through the disasters of 2020, that I need friends I feel intimately safe with to share my unfiltered thoughts and opinions. If I feel the need to filter or hold back because I fear you will judge me or go into a defensive posture when we don't share the same viewpoint, that isn't sustainable. I hate the way I feel inside when I am filtering my language to keep the peace or avoid conflict. An inner circle friend can listen to me vent, challenge me with their different perspective if they disagree, or empathize with shared frustrations. They have no agenda for trying to get me to think the same way as them. They can listen to me and know that I will listen to them.

I need them to see my highest self. Part of life's never-ending process is aspiring to grow. Aspiring to unleash our favorite selves. I am deeply vested in this work. The people in my life who can see past my surface level, past my shadows, past my insecurities, and speak to the real me are keepers. The people who are distracted by my flaws and areas where I struggle do not get to be an inner circle. They will bring out my worst qualities, not my best.

The last thing is that my inner circle friends must be people I deeply admire and respect. Jim Rohn coined the phrase, "You are the average of the five people you spend the most time with." However, multiple studies[18] looked at how people are impacted by the people around them and found that the number is much, much wider than five. It even trickles out to the second and third degrees. Meaning we are also impacted by the people our friends are spending time around.

I have to be totally fine with the idea that if we keep hanging out, I may end up having some of your characteristics, thoughts, or behaviors rub off on me. If you are going to bring me down, not help me rise up, this isn't sustainable.

And then, I also look at how I can give. Will I be able to love you the way you want to be loved by your friends?

I rarely ever do phone calls. Calling just to chit-chat or say something that could have been a text or email is not my jam. We can plan an appointment on my calendar to catch up on the phone, video chat, or talk in person. I would absolutely love that. But I don't show love via spontaneous phone calls. We will give each other anxiety.

I recently had two friends go through horrifically challenging times, and each was flung into single motherhood without warning. I signed up for the meal train. That seemed like the least I could do. Later on, I recalled to my friend Laura how miserably I failed at both experiences.

It would take too long to explain the details, but the short version is it involved a panic attack in the grocery store, getting distracted, and both of them ended up with gift cards in their email inbox. Laura said to me, "Sophia, if we ever live near each other again and there is a meal train going around for me, you are the last friend I would ever expect to sign up. I would much prefer you to take that time and energy you were going to spend, come sit on my couch with me, and help me strategize and process what I'm going through."

"YES! I am THAT friend," I said. Ironically, one of the friends who got a gift card in her inbox has literally had me do this, and we are still mapping out her game plan back to stability and calm.

I don't cook, host dinner parties, drink alcohol, go to loud places with big crowds, or do small talk. I don't enjoy shopping. I will talk about spirituality, politics, social issues, and any type of personality profiling system that has been invented. I have a loud voice that carries in a restaurant. I'm direct and assertive but not mean. If you don't assert your needs, I will likely cross over your boundaries because I didn't know they were there. I will constantly push you to step out of your comfort zone toward your dreams. All that said, I'm not the ideal friend for a lot of people. I'm now hyper-aware that this two-way street has to work both ways, for me and for them.

The Courage to Communicate

The work I am currently doing in my friendships is growing the courage to communicate my needs and growing my skillset to see my people better.

My friend Lee Anne has also been working on this same growth. We had been acquaintance friends for a long time, but thanks to Instagram stories and DMs, it was becoming more and more apparent that we had a ton in common and were working on similar passions. After a couple of walking dates, she bravely said to me, "Here's the deal. I like you a lot. I want to invest in a friendship with you, but I am at max capacity. I have no room to invite more people into my world who are not as committed to friendship as I am. You are the type of person I would like to have in my inner circle, but I don't know if you want the same thing or what that would even look like. I only have the bandwidth to invest in the friendships that are serious right now in my life."

Are. You. Kidding. Me? Fireworks might as well have gone off in my heart. I could hear the birds singing in the trees. She is also direct and assertive? Is she communicating her needs to me? She has been a safe space for my inner world and wants to put me in the same category I want to put her? And we're going to talk about it? Is this real?

We went on to have an amazing conversation about our friendship needs, what has hurt us the most in the past, and how we like to receive love. For her birthday a few weeks later, I decided my gift to her was going to be a questionnaire.

In friendships that have longevity or close proximity (like school friends, neighbors, or coworkers), we can learn the little nuances about others. But for most people, it's hard to see the details of their lives. I thought back to those days with the hospital visit or the kids being born. What if someone knew exactly what drink I wanted from Starbucks? What if someone knew what meal to bring my family for dinner that everyone would eat? How seen would I have felt?

Then, I started thinking of the future. What if I'm shopping and see something that screams about her personality? What size do I buy? What if I want to surprise her with something? Who are her other people? Shit. I don't even know how many siblings she has. I would probably have to scroll social media to know how to spell her kids' names correctly.

I made a list of all the things I wanted to know about her so I could learn how to see her. I plan to work on growing this information in more of the friendships in my life. I want to get better at making sure they know I love them. I want to show my people my love for them by truly seeing them.

I've included a free download of this list in the app for you if you want to grow your ability to see your friends better. It's my expectation that you will customize it and curate your own version of how you want to see and love people. This document isn't exhaustive. It's meant to hand you a starting point and inspire you to join me in learning how to see people better.

Forgiveness and Love

I also asked myself, what do I do with all these friends that don't meet these crazy high standards I'm setting? It's quite simple. I love them all.

I cannot mentally manage dozens of databases and keep up with the intricacies of everyone's life who I call a friend. I needed to find the easiest way to do this. First, I internally forgave all of the pain from the past. It's even easy for me to forgive the pain of the present. When I look at what happened each and every time I hurt someone I loved, it was never intentional. I was too distracted by my own thoughts, life, and balls I was juggling to have the capacity to slow down and consider how they may receive my action or inaction. I choose to tell myself a story that everyone else has the best of intentions and loves me as well.

If someone, somewhere out there, intended to hurt me with passive-aggressive behavior and was trying to send a message to me with their neglect or choice of words, they were only hurting themselves. My life is filled with so much joy when I choose to fill in the gaps of information with stories that give everyone the benefit of the doubt.

I have learned to meet people where they are in the season they are in. I once believed that close friends were always for life. That led to some intense pain when seasons shifted, and the friendships grew apart. At one point, I adopted a belief that most friendships are for a season, but an exclusive, short list of people are friends for life. That also didn't work out when that shortlist became seasonal.

Now I've said to hell with all of that. It's too confusing. As life keeps ebbing and flowing, I've noticed that it can be quite fluid. Based on what everyone is going through, what we share in common, and what's happening in our personal and professional lives, intimacy may come and go. I've watched friendships drift away and then reemerge. I've watched friendships that I thought were impenetrable fade. Now, I don't give this much thought or energy.

The people who are currently showing up, are emotionally safe and responsive, see me for the real me, and have admirable qualities—they get a seat at my table. The people who drifted away may come back when it's right. You are welcome to disagree with my approach. I'm not offended. If it doesn't resonate with you, it's because you have a different definition of a ten. You may have more capacity to invest in more people. You may need different qualities in your friends.

I've been asked before how to have "the talk" when a friendship is ending. The only time I've ever had a talk was before I understood all of these seasonal transitions. In retrospect, I did more damage than good. That was over fifteen years ago. Now I relax into whatever it is. I just observe what is happening, what feels natural, and try not to force something that isn't in alignment.

I deeply love all my friends from all my seasons and always will. Right now, in this season of life, I have extremely small pockets of time to dedicate to this spoke. Like, really, really, really small. So, I decline almost every invitation I receive, usually so I can be home to tuck my kids into bed, have dinner together with the four of us, or sleep in and make chocolate chip pancakes. A yes to anyone for the evening is a no to seeing my child at all that day because he's in daycare until 5:00 p.m.

I don't have to have any conversations with people because no one has harmed me in some way that I feel like I need to have a breakup talk. As I mentioned in the spiritual spoke, I try to focus on what I am running toward, not what I am leaving behind. How can I make more time for these people I love so much? Where can I squeeze in an evening away? Who do I need to check in on because it's been too long? I just move toward who I want to love more and trust the process to work itself out.

If this seems like it would be hard for you to navigate, you may need to read the book I recommended in the last chapter, *Set Boundaries, Find Peace* by Nedra Glover Tawwab.

Earlier, I mentioned that I still enjoy the band Hanson. Most people think of them as a one-hit wonder for their song MMMbop from 1997. I don't know how these brothers managed to write these lyrics as adolescents, but reading them in my late thirties hits different. Imagine how much pain and suffering we could have spared ourselves if we had heeded their warning:

FRIENDSHIP

You have so many relationships in this life
Only one or two will last
You go through all the pain and strife
Then you turn your back and they're gone so fast...
... so hold on the ones who really care
In the end they'll be the only ones there
And when you get old and start losing your hair
Can you tell me who will still care?

...in an Mmmbop they're gone...

...Plant a seed, plant a flower, plant a rose
You can plant any one of those
Keep planting to find out which one grows
It's a secret no one knows
It's a secret no one knows
Oh, no one knows

MMMbop...

Beyond the Circle

Does this mean I only show up for my limited inner circle? Absolutely, positively not. Whenever I am aware of a need, and I have the capacity to give or help, I will.

There's a Daniel Tiger episode that I feel explains this concept the best. If you're unfamiliar with this toddler TV series, it's a modern-day animation spin-off from Mister Roger's Neighborhood.

In one episode, a big storm comes through their town and creates a lot of damage. Daniel's parents explain to him that, first, you check on your family. If they're okay, then you check on your neighbors. And once you know they're okay, you check on the community. When Daniel feels scared seeing all the debris, his father tells him to look for the helpers. Whenever something terrible happens, you can always find the helpers.

If I were to write a translation for this book, up to this point, it would be this:

(Self-care) First, check on yourself. Are you okay? If you are not okay, please seek the help you need first. We can't help you if we don't know something is wrong. You can't help others if you are not well.

(Family) Next, check on your family. Is everyone ok? If someone in your family is not okay, they are your next priority. It's okay if everything else must wait while your family gets on stable ground again. There is no reason to feel guilty if you are in a season of survival and can't show up to help everyone else because your family requires everything you have right now. And remember from the last chapter, your definition of who is family is unique to you.

(Friends, inner circle) Then, our inner circle. I don't keep tabs on whether it's been days, weeks, or months since I've connected with my core people. Life can be hectic. But I know that when I am okay and my family is okay, I am reaching out and checking on these folks to make sure they're okay. I am encouraging them to be brave enough to ask me for help when they are not.

(Friends, in general) After that, I have such a long list of people I love and care about. If there's anything I can do to help them, support them, or encourage them, I will. But I have learned to be mindful not to do it at the expense of my first three priorities.

And lastly, my community. (This is the perfect transition to the next chapter.)

Chapter Eleven:

CONTRIBUTION

This right here is why everything else matters.

Contribution.

How will we leave this place better than we found it?

Every single spoke on the wheel of life is connected to our contribution.

Every single one of your lives is a necessary puzzle piece in our shared humanity. We need you. We don't just need you here physically, but we need you plugged into the right spot where you belong. We need you to be aware of your unique shape and the unique designs you have to offer. Being aware of yourself will be the only way that we can find where you belong in the puzzle.

What happens if you build a puzzle but one piece is missing? It will forever feel incomplete.

CONTRIBUTION

What happens if you try to force yourself into a spot where you don't belong? It will throw off everyone else's ability to find their proper positioning.

So, tell me...

How do you want to contribute to this world?

If you are uncertain of your vision of a ten in this spoke, think back to so many questions that have already been asked here. The more you go inward, the more you will know where you belong out there.

In the spiritual spoke, we examined what lights your soul on fire.

In the career spoke, we asked, what are your unique strengths?

In the financial spoke, we reflected on whether your values are integrated with the decisions you're making for many areas of your life.

In the self-care spoke, we examined what exhausts you and what fuels you.

In the friendship spoke, we considered the question, what are the quirky ways you enjoy spending your time? And with which types of people?

I could keep going, but you get the point. Now, let me add a couple of new questions,

What pain is crushing your heart the deepest right now?

Is there a problem you see in the world that bothers you immensely?

You probably won't be able to solve it. Certainly not alone. But you can begin to question, "What is one small action I can take?"

I love the quote, "Be the change you want to see in the world." It's credited to Mahatma Gandhi, but that's actually a paraphrase of the words he wrote in a 1913 journal article[19] or the *Indian Opinion*. It may surprise you to learn that he was writing about how to treat snake bites when he penned these words: "We but mirror the world. All the tendencies present in the outer world are to be found in the world of our body. **If we could change ourselves, the tendencies in the world would also change. As a man changes his own nature, so does the attitude of the world change towards him.** This is the divine mystery supreme. A wonderful thing it is and the source of our happiness. We need not wait to see what others do."

The smallest action we can take is to first align ourselves with our own integrity. Choosing our values, living according to them, and allowing the ripple effects of that to begin to filter.

As we clarify our values, we can discover our favorite selves. When we begin to unleash her, him, or them into the world, we will shift the definitions of every spoke for others. We will create new examples of how life can be lived.

As we begin showing up as our favorite selves and living according to our values, we will have more clarity around where our strengths lie and how we can best contribute to affecting real change.

CONTRIBUTION

Think Global, Act Local

Long ago, I heard the mantra— think global, act local. It struck a chord with me.

Around 2016, many of us felt the world shifting. Things were changing in America, where I live. Political discussions moved from a social faux pas to a categorizing system. Us versus Them was growing, and we watched it escalate. Institutions, systems, and oppressors were all under attack. The years that followed carried a heaviness for many. Constant headlines and social media posts brought to light large national and international debates.

Much of that anxiety and discord was absorbed by our bodies, our friendships, and our familial systems. We saw firsthand how issues at the macro level were deeply affecting our microcosms.

On one specific day in 2017, I was particularly disturbed. My body had absorbed as much as it could take, and I hit my breaking point. I attempted to "educate" or "inform" myself about the national events by watching something on the news, but it overwhelmed me. All I could hear on the other side of that screen was fear being shouted into the world. Fear for our country. Fear of fellow humans. Fear. Fear. Fear.

I canceled my lunch date, crawled under the sheets of my bed and lay there weeping. I wept because I saw so much beauty. I saw so much kindness, goodness, and humanity. How were the people in power and the people with influence missing all of this? How was the world I was living in so different than the one they lived in? I wept for over an hour in the fetal position under my bedsheets.

Those who know me well know this isn't my normal behavior. I will never forget sitting up on the side of my bed, planting my feet on the ground, and saying to myself, "No more."

I remembered that the opposite of fear is love. I was taught this at a young age in the scriptures. 1 John 4:18 says, "There is no fear in love, but perfect love drives out fear." I remembered that I had been learning about the emotional vibration chart. Fear is near the bottom, but love is near the top.

My husband and his friend Nate were standing in the kitchen. I was pissed. Poor Nate. He had never seen me in a rage. I had clearly been crying, and I came out and told them what I heard on the news that triggered me to my breaking point. I said to them, "I can't take this anymore. I have to feel like I am doing something, so I am going to love harder. I am going to love deeper. I am going to double down on loving others as much as I can handle to make my small difference in being the opposite of this fear that is taking over our world."

I had spent years saying, "One day, when I have more time, I would love to be a Guardian Ad Litem." I had told several people I know, "You should really be a Guardian Ad Litem! You would be so great at it! It's such a great program!" Now I know that shoulding on other people is just a reflection of your value system. It was me who was supposed to volunteer.

A Guardian Ad Litem in Florida is a voice for the child in the foster care system. Other states have different names, such as CASA (Court Appointed Special Advocate). GALs visit children in foster care at their placements and also dive into everything else in their lives. They may meet with their teachers, their daycare centers, their doctors or anyone involved in the child's life. And then, in court, they are the voice for the best interest of the child. Most GALs are volunteers. I cannot speak for other states, but in Florida, there are nowhere near enough volunteers for every child to have a voice. In Hillsborough County, where I live, around 50% of the children have a GAL.

That day in my kitchen, I signed up to learn how to be the voice for a helpless child. That was the start of a new season in my life. I spent the next three years as a GAL and the next six years deeply immersed in community involvement.

A few weeks after that moment in the kitchen, I learned about a non-profit organization in the community, only one mile from my home. It is a literacy non-profit that teaches non-English speaking adults how to read so they can help their children in school, get a G.E.D., and find better employment. While the parents are getting educated, their toddlers are in another room learning so they can be prepared for kindergarten. Their mission is to use literacy and education to empower the entire family. I discovered that they were doing incredible work to break families out of the poverty cycle but were on the brink of closing due to a lack of finances and community awareness. A spark lit inside me. I scheduled a meeting with Angelica, the Executive Director, a woman I've come to know as one of the most incredible humans on the planet. I mentioned her story in Chapter 4. After learning more about their work, I looked her in the eyes and said, "I will make it my mission to shine a flashlight on you. You will no longer be the best-kept secret in this community."

Five years later, we built a strong board of directors. She went from being in the red, to breaking even, to a three-month emergency fund. She went from a small, undersized, slightly unsafe location to a new home for the center that was perfect. She went from an unknown name to being well-loved and embraced by the community. Her staff is now strong and thriving. All of that, put together, means that lives are changed each day.

These were things that broke my heart. Powerless children. Uneducated adults, and children. And it turned out there were puzzle pieces that needed to be placed in my own zip code. It was my responsibility to find my appropriate positioning.

Think back to the Daniel the Tiger reference. Once you, your family, and your friends are okay, lift your head up and check on your neighbors. Of the issues that break your heart, are there people in your own zip code who need a helping hand?

Your Strengths

Circling back to the CliftonStrengths assessment referred to in the career chapter, understanding my strengths was instrumental in helping me figure out where my contributions were best invested.

I took the test for the first time in January 2017, and my number one strength was activator. I get the ball rolling. Number two is strategic thinking. Also, in my top five at that time were futuristic, which is visionary thinking, then connectedness, which is connecting people together. My number five was arranger, which simply means my brain thinks like a chess board, understanding what needs to go where to achieve the end goal.

If you put these pieces together, it shouldn't surprise you that I am the rare type of person who actually loves board meetings. I love sitting around a table, collaborating to determine the best ideas and next steps. I'll sit through a meeting about writing bylaws, understanding the impact it will have in future situations.

My parents were always hands-on people. My mom is the person who shows up with a pot of chicken soup anytime someone says they are sick. My parents, both Louisiana-born, are known for their gumbo or jambalaya anytime there is a potluck or reason to celebrate. Both my brother and sister became public school teachers. Throughout my entire childhood, it was normal for us to have an extra person living in our home for one reason or another. My parents have taken in so many stray or abandoned animals over the years and nursed them back to health. Giving and serving were modeled for me as something that is done at the ground level. If you're not getting your hands dirty, you're not working.

But there I was, not feeling like I was getting my hands dirty. I burn most meals. I am the opposite of the hostess with the mostest. I am the hostess with the leastest and have to borrow dishes to host my kids' birthday parties.

Learning about each person's unique gifts was so life-giving for me. You need the frontline workers of any non-profit organization who actually provide the service. But their work can't happen if someone doesn't start a non-profit, find the funding, and recruit the right people into the right roles. Remember, in the puzzle, we all belong, just not in the same spots.

What are your strengths? How can you use those unique skills to contribute to the world? Is it your family that needs you? Your neighborhood? Your town? An internet-based community? Does your best work birth itself when you're alone in seclusion creating your craft?

There are no right or wrong answers to these questions. The work is aligning yourself with where you belong.

Seasons

When you think of your ten in the contribution spoke, I encourage you to consider your season of life. Think back to the end of the most recent chapter. Giving to others should not come at the expense of self-sacrifice. It comes from a place of abundance because you are okay, your family is okay, and your friends are okay.

I have seen phenomenal humans give so much that they burn out. We don't want to lose you on the battlefield. We are all playing a long game here that will outlive the generations currently alive. This work is so much bigger than you, so please don't overextend yourself.

Seasons can also look different based on other moving parts in your life, whether or not you have children, where you live, or the emotional bandwidth of your job. There are so many careers that require the entirety of someone's bandwidth to fulfill their duties. I think of my friend who is an ER nurse, the public-school teachers we know, and our friend who is an EMT. He may sometimes be the first to the scene of a fatal car accident. If your work requires you to constantly pour out, we need you all to please, please, please prioritize taking care of yourselves. Our society depends on you to refill your cup so you can stay on the front lines rather than burn out.

Your contribution may directly overlap with your career, and that's beautiful and fine if it does. If you are a full-time, stay-at-home parent, the level of overstimulation you feel at the end of the day may mean that those little ones are your max capacity. I think of those caring for aging or ill loved ones, and the pockets they have for their self-care are so rare, much less being able to take on a cause. That one life may be their entire contribution spoke right now.

For me, personally— I can feel I am in the middle of a season of transition. I've been through enough of them that I recognize this uncertainty and lack of clarity. From 2016-2021, I felt the Divine calling me to invest in my roots. My work centered around my hometown, family, and community. Throughout 2022, I pulled away from five different boards I had poured much of my heart and soul into for five years. I know I'm moving up from the roots to growing my stem. I'm not sure what is on the other side of this season, but I will know when it's time to birth the fruits.

My definition of a ten in this spoke is that I am maximizing my unique gifts and talents to leave this world better than I found it.

Right now, writing this book, healing myself, serving my clients, and caring for my family is my max capacity. My contribution outwardly is scaling back and turning inward for now, and I'm perfectly at peace with that.

What season are you in?

Their Favorite Selves

Do you know what one of the most challenging parts of people setting out to live their favorite lives after reading this book will be? **The way others respond to them when they start changing.**

If we want this free life for ourselves, then are we willing to expand to a place where other people can be their favorites selves around us too?

If you are uncomfortable with someone wanting to marry who they love, why? If you're uncomfortable with someone choosing to have nine kids, why? If you are uncomfortable with someone changing their name or how they dress, why? Or styling their hair a unique way, practicing a different religion than you, or homeschooling their kids— ask yourself why. Do you get uncomfortable if someone tells you they are choosing to have no kids or stay single? Why? Or here's one I see a lot, folks critical of body positivity from people in large bodies. Why? I've watched the internet shame women who have a disability and choose to become mothers. Why? If someone's definition of living their life at a ten is different than yours, but it's not causing any harm to others, why does it make you uncomfortable?

If you regularly find yourself uncomfortable with the choices other people are making for themselves, I encourage you to embark on this work. Find the answer to "Why?" Getting curious and diving in can teach you so much about yourself.

What triggers you? By trigger, I mean what is something that someone says or does that can shift your emotions on a dime. Different behaviors may elicit different responses, but common reactions are finding yourself defensive, angry, annoyed, anxious, critical, or disgusted whenever this behavior arises in others. Start asking why and looking inward. It's one of the best gifts to give yourself because it will reveal so much about you.

Nowadays, it takes a lot to trigger me, but I used to be very susceptible. In the past, I had many responses I didn't realize were me "being triggered." If I want to encourage you all to do this work, then I feel like one of the most helpful things I can do is give you an example. But please understand that this work is often very vulnerable and revealing, so writing about this is highly uncomfortable.

One example of me healing a trigger is that in college, I had three classmates across different classes who got deeply under my skin. I was annoyed whenever they spoke. My skin would crawl when they would bust out in one of their jokes that I didn't find funny. I am not sure whether 20-year-old Sophia hid her eye rolls or not. Remember that college professor from Chapter 6? I used to stop by as often as possible during his office hours to pick his brain. One day, he said to me, "We only judge others for what we judge ourselves for." It was the first time I heard that statement, so I asked myself, "What is something you are highly judgmental towards others about?"

I pondered that question for the rest of the day. I thought of these three different individuals who got under my skin. What did they have in common? Once I saw the overlap, I couldn't unsee it, and it made me sick to my stomach. All three of them were loud and boisterous, and all three of them were in large bodies. My two greatest insecurities about myself. More than any other traits about me, I was criticized and picked on for being overweight and being "too loud" or "too much." When I interacted with people who embodied my insecurities, it felt like nails on a chalkboard.

Over the coming weeks, months, and years, I had to clean that up. "The work" didn't involve them whatsoever. It involved me healing within. As I tamed my inner critic and grew some self-love, I healed the way I perceived others. When I chose to look at these individuals with love and try to enjoy their humor, I gave permission to myself to also enjoy being the center of attention in a room.

Most of my triggers I have been able to identify and heal just by noticing the patterns and becoming aware. However, as recently as last year, I noticed I was overreacting to some comments that would go on to bother me for days. I couldn't identify the pattern, so my sweet husband, after listening to me vent to him AGAIN about frustrations said, "If I could help you through this, I would, but I think it's time for you to get back into therapy. I think you need a professional." That's when I decided to try EMDR for the first time. I thought I went to ask for help to stay calm and not get easily upset. I didn't know that I was actually signing up to look at decades worth of grief that had been buried and unresolved. That was why I couldn't draw a line or make sense of why I was getting upset. I share that to say— sometimes we can do this work ourselves and other times, we need to ask for help.

Why did I decide to write about triggers in the contribution spoke? Because healing yourself truly is one of the kindest things you can do for others. At the start of this chapter, I referenced the Gandhi quote, "Be the change you want to see in the world." Do you want to live in a world where people accept you? Do you want to live in a world where you feel free to be your authentic self? Do you want to live in a world that feels supportive? Me too. It requires all of us to start in the mirror.

Different Food in the Fridge

Around 2016, I realized that I had a lot of internal work to do again. Different events made me hyper-aware of my biases I hadn't previously seen (we all have biases—it's part of human nature.) Because I'm a naturally curious person, I started picking up some books to help me understand the world through different lenses. I saw something about the statistics of how few of the published books from major publishing houses were written by women, people of color, and specifically women of color, and I was floored. I went over to my own bookshelf, Kindle app, and Audible app to see who all had influenced my worldview.

It felt like a punch in the gut.

Except for Brené Brown, all the books I had read in the previous ten years that shaped my perspectives of business, relationships, spirituality, finances, and everything else I had been studying were written by white men. This is no dig at them. I'm really, ridiculously thankful for the content I learned from them. I still revere many of them as some of my favorite authors.

The point is that I was missing substantial chunks of voices and perspectives. So, I started looking for more content from female authors, men and women of color, the LGBTQ community, and people with disabilities. When I couldn't find books, I found people on social media to follow. I absorbed their content there. Holy moly. Had I been living with my head in the sand or what?

What I learned from those authors was that my experience was very different from theirs. Their memoirs, narratives, and stories opened my eyes to experiences I had never encountered because I had only consumed content with people who shared similar lives to mine.

One of the most moving statements I heard in my mid-twenties was, "Make friends with people who have different food in their refrigerator than you do" (I cannot recall or find where I heard it). I looked around and realized that most of my friendships were with people who dressed like me, ate like me, had religious beliefs like me, and much more. It was my loss. I worked to open my world.

What I learned was that I had barely scratched the surface of the beauty that is in this world. I was missing out on so much richness and depth that can be experienced when we expand our network.

You know what else happens when we expand our network? We are no longer in an echo chamber of people who think the same way, behave the same way, and agree with us constantly.

As we seek to grow our contribution spokes and make significant contributions to the world, I challenge you to look around at the tables you are building. The rooms you are designing. Who are you inviting in? Are you surrounded by like-minded individuals and people who agree with you constantly? Or are you surrounding yourself with people who have different experiences, backgrounds, perspectives, personalities, and views so that you are regularly being challenged in a healthy, supportive way?

Giving and Receiving

If you listen to anyone's story, it's usually a combination of hardship and blessings. There are many things to be grateful for, mixed up with pain and heartache from when life delivered blows.

Imagine if we were all living in an intentional way to use our gifts, talents, resources, and networks to alleviate the pains of others. Sometimes we would be the givers, and sometimes we would be the receivers. I believe this is the natural flow of the universe. To learn how to give and receive. For many, one side of that coin is easier than another.

If you are a natural giver and are always trying to help others, do you find it uncomfortable to receive? When someone pays you a compliment, do you immediately deflect? This may sound like,

Person: "Oh my gosh! I love your shirt!"

You: "Oh, this ol' thing? It's like ten years old," or "Thanks! It got it on clearance for $5!" or "Thank you! And look at your shoes. OH my gosh! LOVE them!"

Holding a compliment with a simple "Thank you," and no other response is highly uncomfortable for many people. This is because receiving can be challenging. It's easier to hear the compliment and then point the energy somewhere else. Practice saying thank you with no follow-up. Just receive.

On the flip side, many others have trouble giving. You have people in your life that are not the most generous. Whether it's their time, money, knowledge, or any resource, they would prefer to keep it for themselves. This may be scarcity; they are afraid there won't be enough. This may be fear. If this is you, practice being more generous in small ways. Leave a disproportionately high tip, support a youth fundraiser in your community, find a cause you care about and volunteer or donate. Create the habit of expanding and opening your heart to others.

When we are all in the flow, able to give and receive, then we are also all lifted higher. Our shared humanity is much stronger when we are not stubbornly independent and self-sufficient but rather recognize we are part of a larger whole and playing our part.

My favorite perspective on this comes from my dear friend Irene. She inspires me constantly. Her wisdom and intelligence are a rare combination. She and her sister grew up the daughters of a single-mother migrant worker. She went on to become a certified public accountant and made partner before she turned thirty. She lives by the motto, "Lift as we climb." She acknowledges that her success is a culmination of many things, including the people in the community who helped her along the way. She sees it as her calling to turn around and lend a hand to someone else behind her while she keeps climbing up the mountain.

We can do both. We can climb our own mountains and help pull others forward at the same time. Sometimes, we may even be the person someone else is trying to reach out a hand to lift up.

Why are the snakes biting?

Remember when I shared at the beginning of this chapter that the Ghandi quote turned out to be about snake bites? Let's understand the connection he was making.

While he does offer some medical advice on what to do if you're bitten, he explains his frustrations with how many people are getting bitten to begin with. That it's completely unnecessary. He explains that society has been conditioned to fear snakes, so much so that the Indian government put out a reward to anyone who kills a venomous snake. Despite the allure of people believing snakes are intelligent, science has proven they aren't.

Their venomous bite triggers when they go into defense mode. When they believe they are under attack, they bite.

Would there be as many people getting bitten by snakes if there weren't as many people trying to kill them for a reward?

He also explains the stories of people who lived very peacefully among the snakes. They went into the wilderness with no weapons and came out alive. They didn't fear the snakes. They didn't attack the snakes. So the snakes didn't attack them. And in that context, Ghandi wrote: "I personally feel that when we rid ourselves of all enmity towards any living creatures, the latter also cease to regard us with hate. Compassion or love is man's greatest excellence. Without this, he cannot cultivate love of God. We come to realize in all the religions, clearly, that compassion is the root of the higher life."

We fear what we do not understand. We can tap into our compassion to have better understanding.

What's Next

Just open your eyes, friends. Where is there room for more compassion in your life? Where, within your own heart or zip code, can you overcome fear with love?

What is something you can do that is in alignment with your unique puzzle piece design? What breaks your heart, and what can you do about it?

It can be as small as donating what you can to a cause that is doing the work that matters in the world to you. It can be as big as starting the next movement. Only you know how your favorite self is being asked to contribute today.

For my extremely empathetic friends reading this, please go back to the self-care spoke and the mind spoke. Remember to manage your energy and your thoughts well. You cannot save the entire world. It's not your responsibility. You are just meant to put your own puzzle piece where it belongs and have faith that there are enough other incredible humans in our shared humanity that will do the same.

Together, we will leave this world a better place than we found it.

Chapter Twelve:

THE BLANK

How to Choose

The last spoke on the *Favorite Life Wheel* is blank.

While working with people to unleash their favorite selves, I found that there was often an area of their lives that took up a lot of mental space but wasn't represented on the wheel.

The beauty of leaving this last spoke blank is that you can customize it to your needs. What is something you are currently working on in your life that you want to measure? These are the most common options I see people apply to their 10th spoke:

- Partnerships/Dating/Romance
- Hobby/Travel/Fun/Pleasure
- Their home (Remodel, Declutter, New Build)
- Education/Learning/Personal Development

- Art/Creativity
- Time Management

I recommend choosing something that you find takes up a lot of space in your mind or that, if it were improved, would have a significant impact on your quality of life.

How to Navigate

Regardless of what you decide for your tenth spoke, you have probably caught onto the template for helping it grow. Here is the guide:

Name the spoke.

- Define that spoke at a 10.
- Evaluate what number on your 1-10 scale you are at today.
- Reflect on what impact this spoke is having on the rest of your wheel.
- Identify habits that will help you grow to your 10.

The Rest of this Chapter

Yes, the 10th spoke is the blank spoke. If that was all I was going to say, then the chapter would end here, but that's not much fun, is it? Instead, I am going to use this space to give you a glimpse into my 10th spoke, which is marriage.

I am fully aware this spoke will not pertain to all readers, which is why the 10th spoke is flexible. Everyone's life is unique, and I want to leave space for you to fill in your own situation. I have clients who have chosen to stay single for the rest of their lives for different reasons. I help them own that and build a gorgeous life that doesn't involve a partner. I also know that some people are taking a break from their romantic life, have decided marriage is not for them, or choose a polyamorous lifestyle. You do you.

For those who are in a marriage or long-term committed relationship or hope to be in the future, I hope you find value in the rest of this chapter. If that is not you, then you can read this chapter to give you some ideas of what you can bring up in conversations with friends or family in the future because you most likely share life with people who are struggling with some of the things I will touch on here.

Luck

My husband and I were eighteen and twenty when we met and were engaged six months later. We were twenty and twenty-two when we walked down the aisle. Most of our friends who got married young, as we did, have had their marriages end in divorce. Ours has never even gotten close. We have changed so much. Those babies who walked down the aisle in 2007 barely resemble who we are now. Fortunately for us, during all that growth, we managed to grow together instead of growing apart. I want to talk through some of the things we have learned over this time.

Before I dive into the lessons we have learned, I want to acknowledge that "mountain" I referred to at the end of the previous chapter we are all climbing. We started our marriage halfway up the hill with no special skill I could teach or pass along.

We both come from homes with parents who are still married and modeled healthy relationship dynamics for us. We were spared having to unlearn toxic relationship habits before getting started.

We both had normal childhoods and escaped any situations of abuse, violence, addiction, neglect, or other major traumas that many other people have to unpack.

If you have ever studied the attachment style theory* in psychology, we both entered the relationship with secure attachment styles. Other than my ADHD, neither of us has any mental health diagnoses personally or in our immediate families that we have to combat while trying to build a marriage.

Many marriages start off rocky or end because of all the history each partner brings into the relationship before it ever begins. As a result, while they are trying to build a relationship, they are also trying to heal themselves and navigate their pasts. This is a lot to place on a marriage, and it is no one's fault if it doesn't work out.

I didn't want to write this chapter with fluffy marriage talk and then create a dialogue in someone's mind that they can use to shame themselves if their marriage didn't work out. You can do everything right, be an amazing partner, and give it your absolute best, and it could still not work out. Please know that this content is meant to help you navigate your future and the things you can control, not the past or what is outside of your control.

---

* There are many resources to learn about this theory. In short, based on someone's upbringing they develop either an anxious, avoidant, secure, or disorganized attachment style that impacts how they interact in future relationships.

The Accidental Event

When my husband and I reflect on our fifteen years of marriage, there is our relationship before 2012 and our relationship after. There really is a stark difference, so let's talk about what happened.

We were in the middle of hustling to build our photography and video production company. I had just left my full-time, well-paying job. We were on our own to create our income. I had the promoter personality, and he was the workhorse behind the scenes.

I joined a local business club at the top of a high rise in downtown Tampa to provide a nicer atmosphere to meet with clients than the local Starbucks. It ended up being a great atmosphere for networking and meeting people in the business community. There was a woman who I frequently encountered there who ran a public relations firm. She was all about promoting her clients and networking on their behalf.

One day, she invited me to a seminar she was hosting for a client. She told me her client was a husband-and-wife psychologist team, and she was looking for vendors to have tables at the seminar, and I could come for free. What I heard was an opportunity to promote my business for free and get to learn new things at the same time. It sounded great. The catch was it was the next two nights. I said yes and started planning right away.

I loaded up my husband's giant iMac 27" computer screen and brought business cards and brochures to promote our wedding photography and cinematography.

The table next to me was The Todd, Tampa's famously well-known adult content superstore. I noticed the banners with the psychologists' faces advertised them as Tampa's best sex therapists. I started to realize I had no idea what I had agreed to that evening.

During the mingling, before the content began, I stood out like a sore thumb. The other vendors were all connected to the sex industry and here I was with a repeating reel of wedding highlight videos. I felt so, so awkward.

To top it off, you must understand Sophia at this time. I was raised in purity culture in the Southern Baptist church. My husband and I were virgins on our wedding night. I had been married for five years and still didn't feel comfortable with my own body. In full disclosure, hubby and I had been to The Todd a few times, but I felt like I absolutely did not belong in that room.

The therapists began their seminar, and we all took our seats. On night one, I learned that sex is all about communication. I learned how improving your sex life is more about making your partner feel safe and comfortable in your presence. They brought in a couple of people to share their stories and experiences about how they keep romance in their relationship fun, exciting, and fresh over the long term. They brought in an original Hooters girl to talk about how she loves her vibrator and what makes for great solo pleasure. Then The Todd people came up and explained all the different choices of vibrators and toys and what they do. They passed out goodie boxes for everyone in the audience, which included a free bullet vibrator, coupons, and sample lubes.

By the end of the night, I drove home in pure shock, with my gift box in the passenger seat, wondering how on earth I got myself into this situation. It was one of the most awkward nights of my life.

However, I came back the next night for part two. At that point, I couldn't blame naiveté. I knew what I was getting into. The motivation to drive over this time had nothing to do with thinking I was promoting my business and going to pick up a potential client. It had everything to do with my sheer curiosity. What else were they going to say?

Once again, I had no idea what I was getting into. Let's suffice it to say that night two was an educational experience I had never been exposed to, and I didn't realize just how naïve I was until that point. I wanted to crawl into a hole. If I thought I didn't belong in the room the night before, I sorely underestimated how uncomfortable I could still feel.

But here is where it got interesting, after they presented all this educational information, the therapists came out and explained that everyone has desires. The difference is not everyone feels safe enough to talk about them. So, most people keep deep, dark secrets of what is happening in their minds. Oftentimes, this causes them to live in shame.

They explained that if you want to improve your relationship, then you must open yourself up to the nonjudgment of another person's fantasies. They said that this does not mean you have to oblige them. No one should ever feel pressured to do something they don't want to do. But what is healthy in a relationship is opening your mind up wide enough to hold space for your partner. Is your relationship safe enough that they can tell you their deepest, most personal, vulnerable thoughts and know you will not respond by laughing at them, belittling them, making fun of them, or punishing them?

I didn't know the answer. Did my husband feel safe enough with me to tell me absolutely anything?

The whole drive home, I prepared myself for the worst. I mean, I just heard stories of people who go into the secret back rooms of the clubs that you don't know you can ask for unless you're in the know. I listened to people talk about things that I am pretty sure I was taught in youth group were a fast pass to hell.

On my thirty-minute drive home, I braced myself. Could I create a fully non-judgmental space for my partner? Could I hear whatever fantasy he may describe and not laugh, squirm, or criticize?

I decided I was ready. I could do it. I needed to hear. I needed to know. That did not mean I would agree to do the thing—it just meant I would listen without judgment.

When I got home, I told him all about everything I learned and then asked him the question. He was visibly uncomfortable. These are not things we talked about in our relationship.

Eventually, we both reached the point of full vulnerability and held space for each other to share what we had never shared. Had those people from the seminar been a fly on the wall, they would have flown out of the window in boredom. If you were reading this chapter thinking I was building up to some kinky reveal about my life, I'm sorry. You are mistaken.

However, what we did do was break through a huge barrier in communication.

It doesn't matter what you share with me. I will not judge you. I will not shame you. I will not laugh at you. You can trust me with your most inner, deepest, personal, and vulnerable thoughts, and I will hold space for you.

I will catch you. No matter what.

Sure, our sex life got better after that, but not because we introduced something erotic into the bedroom. It was better from then forward because we were healthier and more intimate in our conversations.

So much of this book is about having the courage to discover your own needs for yourself and then express them to those around you. Knowing those needs for ourselves is hard enough, much less talking about them.

My husband and I consider our anniversary the day we met. We fell in love because we had deep, intimate conversations about philosophical ideas, art, religion and many other soulful topics. We have always had great communication and dialogue in our relationship, but the level of vulnerability that discussion opened up took our marriage to the next level of feeling safe and secure with another person.

Because of the deepened level of trust that experience created, the last decade has been richer. When we are wrestling with challenges in our lives, make mistakes, embarrassed, or are experiencing shame, we have a certainty that the other person can always be trusted.

The Venn Diagram

The other aspect of our marriage that I know is very unique compared to most people I talk to about relationships is the level of independence we have. My husband and I share very few common interests.

He is into video games, fantasy football, comics, movies, sci-fi, time travel, space, and a host of other things I have no desire to discuss. I am into spirituality, politics, personal growth and development, making dream boards and analyzing personality profiles. I live 70% of my headspace in the future and must regularly be brought back down to reality.

Together, we love dreaming, pursuing those dreams, traveling, and having deep conversations. He's a phenomenal listener, and I have a lot of words I need to get out each day.

Neither one of us expects the other to conform. We have cultivated completely different friend groups, found others to dive into our hobbies with, and fully support our partner having regular nights of fun while we stay home with the kids.

And are you ready for this kicker? It could be a chapter in and of itself. After our daughter was born, we stopped sleeping in the same bedroom. Eight years later, we still have our own rooms.

It started out because it made breastfeeding so much easier. When pregnant, I asked for this arrangement. I knew I was going to nurse, which meant he couldn't help. I wanted him to always have a full night's rest because I didn't see the benefit in two sleep-deprived parents. I said, "My job is to take care of her, and your job is to take care of me." He managed all the household chores, kept the food prepped for us, and would bring me my water and snacks on demand. It worked for us.

But here's what happened over time. We kept getting better sleep apart than together. We spent our first seven years fighting over covers, temperatures, snoring, and alarm clocks. In separate bedrooms, we both got better rest. For the first couple of years, I kept sleeping in my daughter's room because I became a co-sleeping mom. But then, when it was time to end the co-sleeping, we just decided to own it. Why pretend for the other people who don't live here?

We separated the closets and called it what it was. We have a three-bedroom house. The three rooms are mom's room, dad's room, and the shared kids' bedroom. Do we know anyone else who does it this way? Nope. Are we on a mission to get others to do it this way? Nope. Do we own our favorite lives? Yep.

Occasionally, people ask about sexy time if we don't share a bedroom. It makes me laugh because let's just use a little common sense here, guys. We have two bedrooms, not zero. In the history of our marriage, we have never been on the same sleep schedule, so there has never been a "going to bed together" in our dynamic.

After the kids go to sleep, it's 50/50 on whether we have alone time or together time. Sometimes, it's watching TV on the couch. Other times, we say goodnight and both go do our independent stuff in our own bedroom. And it's lovely. I am writing this chapter right now around 10 pm on a weeknight. The kids have been asleep since 8:30p.m. My husband is in his room doing that gaming thing with his friends on the headset that I don't understand, and I am curled up in comfy pajamas in my bed, writing. We have curated spaces and environments conducive to our taste. We are both at such high levels of joy.

In full disclosure, our dream house would have five bedrooms. We would love for each kid to have their own room, for us to each have our own room, but to also have a master bedroom that we do share. It is nice to share a space with your partner. I get it. We do it on vacations and every now and then at home. But it's also so lovely to have our own private space to be alone.

I describe our marriage as two interconnected rings. We are deeply bonded together. We've been apart for a month at a time several times in our marriage (work-related), and we don't like it. We are better together. However, when you look at the two rings from a 2D perspective, it looks like a Venn Diagram. There's his life, my life, and our shared life. I believe that the level at which we respect each other's independence has helped our relationship immensely.

Helping Others

Many of my clients have come to me with relationship issues over the years. It's very common for their 10th blank spoke to be related to their partnership or romantic life. Let's discuss a few common conversations that come up on our calls.

Fix you first: Sometimes, people come to me wanting help to decide whether to stay or leave a relationship. I won't answer the question because only they can answer that for themselves. My approach is always to fix you first. Control everything you can control to get all your other spokes high. Is your self-care low? Let's fix that first. How's the mind spoke? How do you feel in your body? Let your partner do what your partner is going to do while you go inward. Without fail (so far), my clients always get off the fence at some point in this process. Sometimes, when they try to start focusing on themselves, their partners sabotage their efforts and impede their growth. They come to their own conclusion that it's not possible to become their favorite self and stay in a relationship with this person. Other times, they discover that once they feel good in their body, have strong mental clarity, and have figured out how to meet all their own self-care needs, suddenly, their relationship issues start working themselves out.

Date Yourself: Other times, I have single clients who would prefer not to stay single. When we do the *Favorite Life Wheel* assessment, if I see several low spokes elsewhere, especially in the self-care area, I encourage them to take a period to date themselves. Instead of pouring their energy into another person, can they take themselves out to a nice dinner? What kind of date would they plan for another person? Can they plan something extravagant for themselves? Instead of holding space for another person and being a great listener, supporter, and encourager, can they learn to manage their mind and do that for themselves? Can they hold space for their own pain? Our thoughts can be so self-deprecating sometimes. Can they learn to manage their mind to the point that they are as kind to themselves as they would be to a new fling? When you enter a new relationship with the other spokes on your wheel at high numbers, you will attract a different type of partner and you will show up differently in the relationship.

Using the stories I shared from my own marriage experience, I may challenge them to reflect on some of these questions:

What from our past is showing up in our relationship?

Are we repeating any patterns that were modeled for us that are not helpful?

Do I feel safe sharing any of my thoughts, feelings, or experiences with my partner?

Does my partner feel safe sharing any of their thoughts, feelings, or experiences with me?

What does our Venn Diagram look like? Are we completely enmeshed together and need to give each other some space? Are we roommates, two people living separate lives under the same roof?

What's Next

Let's circle back to the top two sections of this chapter. Some parts are worth repeating because they are your next steps.

Of all the spokes, I can provide you with the least guidance here because I cannot know what you choose to declare as your tenth spoke. Only about a third of my clients choose relationship-oriented categories. There are so many other facets to a favorite life you can use this spoke to design. For inspiration, you can refer to the beginning of this chapter, where I gave several examples of what else could be your tenth spoke.

What is something you are currently working on in your life that you want to measure? Also, ask what tenth spoke would help me create the quality of life I crave? Am I hanging on to any part of an inherited definition that I have internalized but doesn't serve me? Is there anything missing from my life that would help me feel whole, fulfilled, and content?

Once you decide what your tenth spoke will be, follow the guide to navigate this spoke. Here is the process once more:

Name the spoke.

Define that spoke at a 10.

Evaluate what number on your 1-10 scale you are at today.

Reflect on what impact this spoke is having on the rest of your wheel.

Identify habits that will help you grow to your 10.

That's it, friends. That's the last spoke on the *Favorite Life Wheel*. I'm confident you will rock this journey to unleashing your favorite self.

Chapter Thirteen:

UNLEASH YOUR FAVORITE SELF

Let's recap the concept of *Unleash Your Favorite Self* and why that phrase is such a powerful rallying cry.

Your Favorite Self is, by definition, something only *you* can declare. There is no should, no supposed to, no expectation implied in the word. It simply means that you tell us what you want for yourself.

So, tell us, who are you, really? Who do you want to be, really? What are the gifts, talents, and skills that you have to offer this world? What protective measures need to be put in place to ensure you have the capacity to share those gifts?

Unleash is a powerful word. It implies that it already exists. It's already inside. You don't need an expert to navigate you in the right direction. You simply need to quiet all the voices and look inward. Most of the answers you need are already there. They are just buried. Suffocating. Drowning. Covered up with fear. Suppressed.

It's time to start removing the layers.

This work is not for the faint at heart. Nor is it a quick turnaround. This work takes time. It takes energy. It takes commitment for the rest of your life.

But what's at stake if you don't start? What's the opposite of "Unleash Your Favorite Self?" I tried to write the antonyms for those words: "Keep caged your disliked self" or "Suppress your people-pleasing self."

It sounds absurd, but it's how so many people are walking around day-to-day. They are living in cages that others built. Meanwhile, the key is hanging around their own neck.

What happens if you open it? What if you have never used your wings before and you crash? What if the world out there is not as safe and protected as your cage?

Well, my dear, that's what this book was about. It's time to learn how to fly. Of course, it will be ugly, messy, and complicated at first, but if the other choice is never knowing what it feels like to soar? I chose the harder path.

The Spokes

I'm fully aware that this book has a lot to process. So many personal development books focus on one key takeaway concept and then spend the rest of the book supporting that single idea. This book is not that. Each chapter could have been a book by itself. Each chapter has people who dedicate their entire lives to one bullet point of what we covered. Let's recap the central messages of the book to connect all the dots:

The Wheel: The *Favorite Life Wheel* is where it begins. If you did the assessment at the beginning of the book, I challenge you to redo it today. Many of you edited some of your definitions or changed your perception of how you view a spoke after you read the chapters. What does your wheel look like now? Which spokes may be neglected or may need a new definition?

Self-Care: Self-care is energy management. Are you giving to others from a place of exhaustion or abundance? Is the way in which you are giving sustainable or taking an irreparable toll on you?

Mind: It starts with our thoughts. Learning how to manage our minds and rewrite our thoughts and beliefs is the foundation for changing anything about our lives. Practice using the Thought Wheel to train yourself how to do this work.

Body: Is the relationship you have with your body healthy? How can you support your body better so it can support you in every other area of your life? What is YOUR definition of health?

Spiritual: How do you look inward? How do you connect with something greater than yourself? What is your purpose? What are your values? Are you living in accordance with them?

Financial: Did you do the Financial Wheel? Are your financial choices in alignment with your values? What needs to change in your financial situation?

Career: How can you best add value to this world? Are you doing it now? Do you want to tie your work to your paycheck or set yourself free from that expectation? Do you know your greatest strengths? Are you using them most days or forcing yourself to cater to your weaknesses?

Family: Which people does this include? Do you need to change anything about yourself to interact in these relationships in a healthier way? What are the next steps you want to take to improve your family life?

Friendship: How do you want to show up for your friends? How do you want your friends to show up for you? Do they know those answers? What actions would breathe more life into your relationships?

Contribution: How can you use your strengths, resources, and gifts to leave this world better than you found it?

Blank: What else would improve your quality of life? What other area would be helped by your choosing to show up more intentionally?

Remember, you don't get the luxury or convenience of neglecting any of these areas. They are all interconnected. When you are suffering in one, it will bleed into all the others. When you improve one, the benefits will reap in all the others. Your life is a culmination of so many components.

Balance

I am not inferring that you need to be perfectly balanced. It rarely happens. Even when it does, it's not sustainable.

These spokes are fluid. They ebb and flow as the dynamics of our lives shift and change. One phone call can change everything about a single spoke and wreak havoc on every other area. I often refer to the wheel as Jell-O, it's always wobbling a little bit.

However, I have found that the stronger each of the spokes becomes, the easier it is to weather those obstacles. There is more support to absorb the blunt force of the unexpected. The higher each spoke, the quicker your recovery.

I'm not out here spreading a message that we are not enough if all the spokes are not a nine or ten. Do not project judgment onto yourself that I didn't imply. The work is the pursuit of your inner freedom. This is the process of creating your favorite life. Part of being human is that it will be messy.

For me, balance isn't the goal. My personal goal is to live with intention. I want to be aware of each of these areas and always in pursuit of growing in each of them. Achieving a ten just means that I have reached the highest vision I can imagine for myself in that area at this time. Sometimes I choose to celebrate the achievement and stay in contentment. Other times, the pursuit of the definition opens my eyes to so many possibilities I didn't realize I could be pursuing, so I choose to raise my own bar.

May you learn to live a life of intention, not of expecting balance.

Habits

In Chapter 2, I promised that at the end of the book, I would tie everything back to habits. I cannot stress strongly enough how much your daily and weekly habits matter. Rather than making a task list of what you need to do to accomplish your goals, a better question would be: What is something small I can do each day to help improve this spoke?

"You'll never change your life until you change something you do daily. The secret of your success is found in your daily routine," says John C. Maxwell, a bestselling author and teacher on leadership. I turned this quote into a motto and changed all the spokes on my wheel by redesigning my entire life, one habit at a time, over many years.

There are so many great books on habits[20]. In my life, changing my daily habits was how I started moving forward from my stagnant position. It's not sexy, and it's not a new idea. It's about as boring as being told you need to get enough water and sleep every day, and yet, we absolutely must talk about it because it's THE THING.

Look at the areas where you scored the lowest numbers on your wheel. Then reflect on the question: What is one daily habit I could adopt in this spoke that would move me closer to my goal?

Sprinkled into every chapter, as I told my story, I modeled habit changes. From figuring out which habits increase and decrease my energy to prioritizing the habits that care for my body, listening to podcasts daily to expand my mind and ideas, to cultivating the courageous habit of having hard conversations.

The most important habit of all the life changes I made was to change how I respond when I feel uncomfortable. Instead of suppressing or ignoring those small signs, I am leaning into the feelings, leaning into the thoughts, asking myself what I need, and then telling the people in my life what those needs are. The habit of listening and advocating for your own needs is at the center of this entire book.

I had already created so much transformation in my life by the time I read BJ Fogg's *Tiny Habits*.[21] His recommendations for habit creation are my favorite because they summarize precisely what I did to effectively create my results.

His three-step formula is as follows:

- Find an anchor moment
- Make the behavior you want tiny
- Celebrate instantly

His book is full of many more research-based, proven tips and tricks for habit change. I cannot recommend it highly enough.

Using the bathroom mirror example from Chapter 4, the anchor moment would be that every day I look in the same mirror to get ready in the bathroom. The behavior I adopted was so tiny. While looking in the mirror, I would say or think my affirmation, "I am beautiful." An instant reward was built into this habit because I was taking a moment where I normally shamed myself and decided to encourage myself.

How can you take the habits you want to create and make them even smaller practices, stacked on top of what you're already consistently doing, and celebrate at the end?

Failure

Many of you are staying in your cages because you fear failing. What if I fall on my face? What if I get hurt? What if I break my leg trying to catch my fall?

Friends, let me tell you right now, all of that will happen. If you read this book, then you know I have fallen on my face. I have failed. I have been hurt so many times. People have hurt me. Disappointment has hurt me. I have hurt myself. I have broken many things that needed time to heal. And guess what? They did.

What if, rather than fearing failure, you embraced it? That's where all the lessons are. That's where the gains are made. It's an inevitable part of the process. There are lessons you must learn that you will only learn when you start trying. Have you ever watched a bird learn to fly? They don't get it right the first time. They strengthen their wings. They experiment a few times until they finally get it right.

Give yourself permission to start experimenting until you figure out what will work…for you. What worked for others may or may not work for you. Start experimenting.

As poet Erin Hanson wrote:

> *"There is freedom waiting for you,*
> *On the breezes of the sky,*
> *And you ask, "What if I fall?"*
> *Oh but my darling,*
> *What if you fly?"*

Putting it into Action

My hope is if you haven't already started using the corresponding journal or app while you were reading the book, that you will now pick it up. It has all the worksheets, tools, exercises, and questions to help you do this work for yourself. If you really want to unlock the maximum impact of what this content has to offer you, I challenge you to dive in. Commit to the process. Put in the work. Accountability goes a long way, so grab a buddy. Do it together. Start a book club for a few months to digest it in chunks.

I don't want you to feel alone on this journey. The last page of this book will connect you to me and our community of support.

May this book be your launching pad. May it be the mirror that helps you realize you are wearing a key around your neck. From this point forward, may you begin the process of unlocking your cage and learning how to fly. I crave to see you soaring.

May you Unleash your Favorite Self!

References

Chapter 1: The Favorite Self

1. FUMITAKE, KISHIMI ICHIRO KOGA. Courage to Be Disliked: How to Free Yourself, Change Your Life and Achieve Real Happiness. ALLEN & UNWIN, 2019.

Chapter 4: Mind

2. Hendricks, Gay. The Big Leap., HarperCollins, New York, NY, 2009.
3. Brown, Brené. Daring Greatly: How the Courage to be Vulnerable Transforms the Way we Live, Love, Parent, and Lead. Gotham Books, 2012.
4. Raichle, Marcus E. "Appraising the Brain's Energy Budget." National Center for Biotechnology Information, U.S. National Library of Medicine, 27 Oct. 2010, www.ncbi.nlm.nih.gov/pmc/articles/PMC124895/.

Chapter 5: Body

5. Robbins, Rebecca, et al. "Examining Sleep Deficiency and Disturbance and Their Risk for Incident Dementia and All-Cause Mortality in Older Adults across 5 Years in the United States." Aging, 11 Feb. 2021, www.aging-us.com/article/202591/text.

Chapter 6: Spiritual

6. "Galatians." The Holy Bible, New International Version.
7. Brown, Brené. Dare to Lead, Vermillion, 2018.

8. Gerber, Michael E., and Hasnah Daud. The E Myth Revisited. PTS Professional, 2010.

Chapter 8: Career

9. Gilbert, Elizabeth. Big Magic, Bloomsbury Publishing, 2016.
10. CliftonStrengths [https://www.gallup.com/cliftonstrengths/] Gallup [https://www.gallup.com/]

Chapter 9: Family

11. Beattie, Melody. Codependent No More: How to Stop Controlling Others and Start Caring for Yourself. Bluebird Books for Life, 1992.
12. American Psychological Association. "Mental Health Treatment Demand Increases During the Pandemic." APA News, 19 Oct. 2021, www.apa.org/news/press/releases/2021/10/mental-health-treatment-demand.
13. HealthPartners. "Stigma of Mental Illnesses Decreasing, According to National Survey." HealthPartners, www.healthpartners.com/hp/about/press-releases/stigma-of-mental-illnesses-decreasing.html.
14. Tawwab, Nedra Glover. Set Boundaries, Find Peace: A Guide to Reclaiming Yourself, TarcherPerigee, an Imprint of Penguin Random House LLC, New York, 2021.
15. Brown, Brené. Rising Strong, Random House US, 2017.

Chapter 10: Friendship

16. "Over Nearly 80 Years, Harvard Study Has Been Showing How to Live a Healthy and Happy Life." Harvard Gazette, 11 Apr. 2017,

news.harvard.edu/gazette/story/2017/04/over-nearly-80-years-harvard-study-has-been-showing-how-to-live-a-healthy-and-happy-life/.
- Waldinger, Robert. "What Makes a Good Life? Lessons from the Longest Study on Happiness." TED, 2015, www.ted.com/talks/robert_waldinger_what_makes_a_good_life_lessons_from_the_longest_study_on_happiness.
17. National Institute on Aging. "Social Isolation and Loneliness in Older People Pose Health Risks." NIA, www.nia.nih.gov/news/social-isolation-loneliness-older-people-pose-health-risks.
18. The Spread of Obesity in a Large Social Network over 32 Years | Nejm, www.nejm.org/doi/full/10.1056/NEJMsa066082
- The Collective Dynamics of Smoking in a Large Social Network | Nejm, www.nejm.org/doi/full/10.1056/NEJMsa0706154.
- Fowler, James H, and Nicholas A Christakis. "Dynamic Spread of Happiness in a Large Social Network: Longitudinal Analysis over 20 Years in the Framingham Heart Study." The BMJ, British Medical Journal Publishing Group, 5 Dec. 2008, www.bmj.com/content/337/bmj.a2338

Chapter 11: Contribution

19. Gandhi, Mahatman. "153. General Knowledge about Health [-XXXII] 12. Accidents: Snake Bite." The Collected Works of Mahatma Gandhi, VOL. 13 : 12 MARCH, 1919 - 25 DECEMBER, 1920, 239-241. https://www.gandhiashramsevagram.org/gandhi-literature/mahatma-gandhi-collected-works-volume-13.pdf

Chapter 13: Unleash Your Favorite Self

20. There are many wonderful books about habits. I personally enjoyed:
- Clear, James. Atomic Habits: Tiny Changes, Remarkable Results: An Easy & Proven Way to Build Good Habits & Break Bad Ones. CELA, 2021.
- Duhigg, Charles. The Power of Habit: Why We Do What We Do in Life and Business. Random House, 2023.
- Fogg, B. J. Tiny Habits: The Small Changes That Change Everything. Mariner Books, 2021.
- Keller, Gary, and Jay Papasan. The One Thing: The Surprisingly Simple Truth behind Extraordinary Results. Bard Press, 2017.

21. Fogg, B. J. Tiny Habits: The Small Changes That Change Everything. Mariner Books, 2021.

MEET
Sophia Hyde

"When you release your favorite self, you set others free too."

– Sophia Hyde

She hosts the weekly podcast Your Favorite Self where she teaches practical ways to apply these principles to day-to-day life, as well as featuring guests who embody the favorite self concept.

Her app, Favorite Self, has resources to help you take this work deeper. The free resources mentioned in this book can be found there. She also offers guided meditations to help you rest, create calm, and look within for answers.

Fun fact, she LOVES speaking engagements. Sophia believes in the power of sharing her journey and knowledge with live audiences. Her passion for inspiring change and transformation is palpable, and her speaking engagements are not to be missed. If you're looking for a dynamic and engaging speaker to inspire and empower your audience, consider booking Sophia for your next event.

After experiencing first-hand what it was like to struggle with overwhelm, work-life balance, and constant guilt, all while quietly going through financial and health stress, Sophia was determined to find a better way to live. In order to unleash her favorite self into the world, she first had to spend years shedding all the "shoulds" the world had layered on her shoulders. Sophia discovered that all the answers she was looking for "out there" had been inside her all along.

Sophia now spends her days helping others create the lives they desire. As a Certified Master Life Coach with ADHD, Sophia specializes in empowering individuals to find their joy while achieving their goals. She offers one-on-one mentorship for a limited number of folks alongside her online courses, live events, and other resources.

Connecting with Sophia is easy. She loves engaging with others on social media where she regularly shares tips, motivational stories, and exclusive content to help you on your path to inner freedom.

Sophia lives in her hometown of Plant City, Florida with her husband and two children surrounded by extended family and her beloved community.

Let's Connect ⊙

www.sophiahyde.com

🅕 🅞 @thesophiahyde

Listen & Follow the 'Your Favorite Self' Podcast

Events & Speaking Engagements hello@thesophiahyde.com